Ernesto Cardenal
LOVE

Ernesto Cardenal

LOVE

Preface by Thomas Merton

Translated by Dinah Livingstone

CROSSROAD · New York

1981
The Crossroad Publishing Company
18 East 41st Street, New York, NY 10017

Published originally as *Vida en el amor*
by Ediciones Carlos Lohle, Buenos Aires
© Ernesto Cardenal 1970

This translation and arrangement © Search Press 1974

Printed in the United States of America

Library of Congress Catalog Card Number: 81-65109
ISBN: 0-8245-0043-1

Contents

Preface

In a time of conflict, anxiety, war, cruelty and confusion, the reader may be surprised that this book is a hymn in praise of love, telling us that 'all beings love one another'.

Perhaps we are too much used to saying that one *ought* to love (thereby giving to understand that, generally speaking, we do not love). We know that there is a *duty* to love, that men have received a *commandment* to love each other. But we take it for granted that they hardly ever obey this commandment. And thus we conclude that the world is evil because there is so little love in it, and we blame and castigate those whom we hold responsible for this lack of love.

Thus a theology or ethics of punishment and retribution takes the place of the vision of love, and love becomes an idealized abstraction. The daily reality of our lives is not under the rule of love, but under the rule of law, of force and of punishment. We talk about love, but we live by hate: we hate in the name of love. In this situation it becomes necessary to assert once more that to love is *not* impossible. Love is not something unreal. On the contrary, love is the *only* reality. Everything that is, is by virtue of love, and if love is not clearly evident in all things, the reason is that we ourselves have made no effort to *see* love in all things. In a very radical sense, love is the only and unique possibility. And everything that is not love is essentially and basically impossible.

The purpose of this book is quite simply to open our eyes to what ought to be obvious but sounds incredible: that 'all beings love one another', that 'all life is love'. This book therefore does not say that men ought to love, nor does it lament the fact that actually men do not love. It does not tell us in great detail how men should be punished for their failure to love. It simply tells us that all things love one another, and it adds that, as a matter of fact, men do love, whether they know it or not. It asserts that men can never cease loving. Even the atheist loves God, unbeknown to himself. If men live in discord with each other and with God, it is not because they do not love, but because they do not understand and accept the fact that they are bound to love of necessity.

Psychoanalysis has taught us that much hate and fear, and even many physical illnesses, are caused by a love which refuses to acknowledge itself as such, a love which has become ill because it fails to recognize its true nature and has lost sight of its object. The conflicts which beset our world are not caused by the absence of love, but by a love which no longer recognizes itself, a love which has become disloyal to its own reality. Cruelty is misdirected love, and hate is frustrated love.

The lucid and 'Franciscan' simplicity of Ernesto Cardenal shows us the world not as we see it, with fear and distrust in our hearts, but as it is in reality. Love is not a dream. It is the basic law of all those creatures who were created free in order to give themselves to others, free to partake of the infinite abundance of life with which God has filled our being. Love is the heart and the true centre of

that creative dynamism which we call life. Love is life itself
in its state of maturity and perfection.

The saints were capable of seeing through the masks that
cover the faces of humanity, and they saw that the masks
are unreal. In the innumerable faces of men they saw only
one face: the face of love (that is to say, the face of Christ).
This is what Ernesto Cardenal has seen and written down.
His entire book is an ever-repeated discovery, an ever-new
poetic intuition of the central reality of life. It is a hymn to
life, and this is why it is so eminently truthful. With the
depth of conviction Cardenal speaks again and again of that
which simply *is*. *Love is*. All else *is not*, because in the same
measure in which things partake of being, they partake of
love. All that is not love, *is not*. All that which is, has its
being and its action in love.

Non-rational creatures are guided by a love which they
do not know, towards an end which they do not understand. For the animal lives in nature without being conscious of it and without that freedom which is the gift of
conscious existence. The animal lives immersed in life, a life
without reflection. We might therefore say that the animal
is 'animated' by life and by love in a passive manner and
without being cognizant of it. The animal has no other
choice than this 'being animated' by its own nature.

This, as Rainer Maria Rilke said in the *Duino Elegies*, is
the reason why the animal is always in immediate contact
with life. Consciousness never intervenes between the animal and life. The animal never reflects on life but simply
lives, and living is its only way of knowing. The animal
does not recognize itself as being live; it simply lives what
it cognizes.

The gift of consciousness is a divine blessing, but it may

turn into a curse if we do not want it to be a blessing. If consciousness as Rilke saw it, were a pure consciousness of love, our love would be as immediate and spontaneous as life itself. As the animal is 'animated' immediately and directly by the life of nature, so we should be activated and motivated in the inwardness of our consciousness by supernatural and divine love. Our consciousness would then not be dimmed by a feeling of frustration, on account of our limitations. It would be a pure consciousness of love, of God, and of life as a gift of love.

The human person, however, is not merely 'animated' or 'vitalized' by his nature. The person is autonomous, conscious of himself, capable of betraying his nature (even though incapable of changing it) and thus capable of either affirming or denying his nature. Man is capable of being or becoming human, whether he likes it or not. He is capable of being a son of God with the full consent of his will or contrary to his will. He can accept himself or reject himself. He is capable of loving his fellow men freely, spontaneously, with complete overtness, or he may prefer to reject and despise them, and in this case he will still love them, even though contrary to his own will. He will love them unknowingly. Thus, even though he still loves, his love has turned against his own self. It has become adulterated, contaminated and disingenuous. That love with which, in the depth of his heart, man wants to open himself to others, turns in upon himself and is locked up inside himself. The love which could and should give nourishment to others, consumes itself. The love which should have found its full realization in self-giving, founders in the confusion and the torment of negation. And it is ironic that negation often hides under the name of love.

Creation in its totality could teach man whom to love if only he were willing to accept its teaching. Life as such is love, and if it is lived in truth, it teaches us to love. But when man's consciousness has been corrupted by the rejection of love, man, who is God's creature, remakes the world in his own image, and the result is a world filled with cruelty, greed, hate, fear and strife. If, on the other hand, man consents to love and gives himself over to life in its pristine purity—life as a pure gift of God—the entire world is overflowing with love.

Isaac of Stella, a Cistercian mystic of the twelfth century, writes:

'This visible world serves man, its master, in two ways: it nourishes him and it teaches him. As a good servant, the world nourishes and teaches, provided that man be not a bad master. A bad master is stupid and wretched; his eyes may be able to penetrate with their glance to the ends of the world and yet see nothing but darkness, and he will then make the world subservient to his body and his stomach. He has no longer any idea why the world was created. He believes that this immense universe was made by God for the sake of his small belly.'

Isaac of Stella was surely aware of the meaning and importance of nourishment, and he was familiar with the joys of festive meals. God has given himself to us in the eucharistic meal, so that man might be capable of communion with God in the gifts of the earth and the fruits of his labour. Isaac knows of the pleasures of wine and of festivity, but he is aware that these are only images of the sublime joy of that love by which God gives to us his Spirit like a 'torrent of delight that inebriates us with a fervour of charity'. Love is for Isaac that divine wine which intoxicates and enraptures us. God wants us to drink of this wine, but we are afraid to do so, notwithstanding his continuous invitation.

This book is filled with invitations to drink and to delight in the banquet of love. Or, to say it much better, it invites us to open our eyes and look at the world around us, so that we may recognize that the festive meal is right in front of us, that the wine, unbeknown to us, is within the reach of our hand.

These basic principles illuminate for us both the creative dynamism of nature and the refreshing and redeeming dynamism of grace. However, these simple principles cannot be acquired in the splendid tepidity of abstract meditation. These pages are filled with the concrete firmness of conviction, because the author wrote them after having completely surrendered to love when he entered a strictly contemplative monastic community, far away from his homeland. Love has its seat not only in the mind or in the heart; it is more than mere thought and desire. Love is action, and it is only in the action of love that we attain to the contemplative intuition of loving wisdom. This contemplative intuition is an act of the highest degree and kind; it is the purest kind of love. And this love does away with the apparent contradiction betwen action and contemplation.

In order to attain to such a mature act of love, we must first have experienced contradiction and conflict. Love is the pinnacle of freedom and of a fully personalized consciousness. And love discovers its own being only in the act of love. A love which acts without being fully conscious of its action, acts contrary to its very nature and does not attain to a full consciousness of self. It remains, as it were, in hiding before itself. Nor is it capable of acting perfectly in accordance with its own nature. The one who acts remains then somehow separated from his love, and his action does not measure up to the fulness of his love. Love here is in contradiction with itself. It rules the heart with a strange and oppressive passion. It carries with it bitterness, anxiety, repression, violence, and even a taste of death. For every love that is not a totally free and spontaneous self-giving, harbours a taste of death. This means then that all our love —the love of us average human beings, who are neither saints nor mystics—is beset with contradiction, conflict and bitterness. And it carries with it a taste of death.

What shall we say of this kind of love? That it should not be? That is is sinful? That it should not be permitted or should be punished? Alas, it is surely true that our poor love tastes of sin. However, Ernesto Cardenal says of it simply that it is *love*, but a love that is not yet sufficiently free, not yet sufficiently pure. And we might add that by what it lacks in being true love we may discover the way that leads to true and perfect love. It is by *accepting this imperfect love, fully conscious of its imperfection, that our love may be made perfect.*

The first step on the way to true and perfect love is the admission that our love, even though not yet pure, is nonetheless love and that by virtue of its very nature it aspires to become pure.

Our moralists sometimes tell us that what is needed is justice, righteousness, honesty, truth and love; that there should be no room for egotism, iniquity and injustice; that egotism should be eradicated and love should be made obligatory.

For the moralist human life is a complex system of virtues and vices, and love is assigned a definite place in the system; it is one of the several virtues. However, the mystic knows of no such complex system; for him love is the one and the all. For him the virtues are different aspects of love, and he holds that the same is true of the vices. The virtues are manifestations of a love that is alive and hale. And the vices are symptoms of an enfeebled love, of a love which refuses to be what it is in its essence.

Actually there is nothing else but love. But this love may live in contradiction with itself. It may at one and the same time be love and hate, love and greed, love and fear, love and envy, love and lust. It is destined, however, to be simply love, without any self-contradictory admixture. And love cannot fulfil its true destiny if we merely try to suppress our hatreds, our greeds, our fears, our jealousies, our lusts. These evil forces receive their strength solely from love. To suppress them is to suppress love. On the contrary, these evil drives ought to be made fully conscious of themselves as love in disguise, and if this is the case, they will not be able to divert the potency of love to the service of that which is not love.

This means that the root of evil and of moral infirmity is ignorance with regard to the kind of love which fails to recognize its true identity and which is therefore blind with respect to its true being and its strength. In the measure in which love begins to become conscious of itself, it recognizes its self-betrayal. It is confused by the spectacle of its radical inner discord. It is frightened by the sight of its divided self and thus becomes the prey of great anguish. For this reason a feeble love prefers to remain unconscious of itself or to know itself only in the form of some disguise. In the degree to which it becomes conscious of itself, it becomes conscious of its inherent contradictions. And thus all our conventional love, if we dare face it, recognizes itself as impure, anguished, divided and burdened with suffering. Such a love is therefore a veritable agony, in the original sense of this term—a tremendous *struggle*. Although God wanted life to be a pure consciousness of love and peace, it is actually a fierce struggle, because in our actual human existence life is the agony of a love which fears to accept itself, aware of the fact that it is self-contradictory, self-affirmation and self-negation at one and the same time. 'He who lives in constant struggle lives in agony, fighting against life itself,' wrote Unamuno.

This, then, is the central problem of every human love. Regardless of how pure love may be, our love is divided by an inherent self-contradiction as long as we are weak human beings, living on this earth and in time. Our love repulses and negates itself. Only God's love is perfectly pure. And human love can only approximate that divine purity in the mystic or the saint who is wholly filled with the love of God. All others (including the one who may some day become a mystic but is not one yet) are bound to live in the anguish of contradiction, or perhaps to be content with a love that is not fully conscious of itself. We experience in ourselves the anguish of this inner conflict from the moment we begin to love. To accept love into our conscious life is to accept simultaneously the consciousness of our agony.

The basic contradiction which love has to face is the contradiction between life and death. A false religious idealism imagines sometimes that it can choose a life without death. Actually, however, to choose life is to choose death, since the temporal life we live as human beings terminates in death. To 'accept' another form of life, one in which we shall never have to face death, is to accept an illusion. An earthly life without death is a mere dream. And even the acceptance of 'eternal life' means for the Christian the prior acceptance of a temporal life that ends with death. Thus death cannot be evaded. It is a part of life, and it actually imparts meaning to life because it involves a basic contradiction that is essential for an understanding of human existence. Why should Christ have died on the cross if death were simply an absurdity? Christ's death rests on the presupposition that every death is tragic. And his death imparts to every death a dimension of hope and of victory. Christ on the cross hallowed the agony of love. The gift which Christ offers to those who love is the cross, and it is this gift which purifies love.

To love life as it really is means to accept it in its total reality, which includes death; to accept not only the *idea* of death but also those acts which anticipate death, in the offering and giving of ourselves.

As Unamuno told us, the materialistic definition of life as a 'conjunction of functions which resist death' makes of life a struggle against truth; and 'a struggle against death and thus also against truth, against the truth of death'.

In a sense, every sacrifice of our personal interest and our pleasure for the sake of another person or simply for the act of 'love' is a kind of death. But at the same time it is an act of life and an affirmation of the truth of life. Every time love accepts a partial 'death', it reaffirms itself as life, triumphs over death and overcomes the self-contradiction of life within us. For this reason love actually demands this intrinsic contradiction to realize itself in our lives.

The metaphysical structure of love is in a certain sense dialectic. Love demands conflict; it nourishes itself by conflict and emerges purified from conflict. But once love attains to its authentic purity in the fire of conflict, it causes the conflict to disappear and with it disappears the contradiction. Thus, even in the midst of conflict, love is able to affirm with absolute certitude: 'All things love each other; everything is love.' And this is not merely an idea but rather the point of a concrete *act*. Without this act, the idea is meaningless.

Love, then, is both action and intuition. And, over and above these, it is a *presence*. It is an act by which our freely offered sacrifice transcends that contradiction of life and death which has its locus in the depth of our being. Love is an act of surrender and the intuition of a freedom beyond life and death, but of a freedom which can only be attained by self-surrender in the midst of self-contradiction. Love becomes perfect in a dialectic of action and intuition, culminating in the mysterious presence of Someone who is invisible but who *is love*. And now we understand that both the act and the intuition of love issue from this presence.

It is of such acts, such intuitions and such presences that these meditations were born, meditations which dare to affirm: there is nothing but love; everything is love. And all that which seems to be distinct from love and which even seems to contradict love, is in reality love. However, in order to see this, one has to love. One has to love wholly, totally, and one has to be willing to accept conflict and contradiction. One has to accept the death of love in order to be able to live the life of love. Once we accept this, we shall see that the conflict disappears and that in reality there is no contradiction, but only love.

What we meet in Ernesto Cardenal's book is more than a systematic doctrine: it is an intuitive knowledge of the profound truth of Christian life. A Christian is united with God in Christ through love. And so this book is entirely traditional—it reminds us at times of St Augustine or of the mystics of 'Bridal Union' of the German Rhineland—and yet entirely modern, bearing resemblance to the vision of Teilhard de Chardin. And it is also absolutely sincere in its great simplicity, a quality which is surely one of the principal signs of the authenticity of spiritual teaching.

Ernesto Cardenal left Gethsemani because of ill-health. However, today I can see that this is not the only reason: it did not make sense to continue at Gethsemani as a novice and as a student when actually he was already a teacher. Today he is an ordained priest and the founder of a contemplative community that lives in the spirit of the wisdom and in the humility of love which are so signally evident in these pages. His community is located precisely at a place where it is most needed—in Central America, where there are no contemplative religious orders. This book, this hymn to life and love, gives testimony of the renewal of the Church in Latin America. It is, we believe, a sign of the dawn of a new day in these countries of the future. They will not only attain temporal freedom and prosperity, but will also learn to sing hymns to life and to love, thus bringing to fruition the abundant potentialities that are still dormant and hidden in that rich, volcanic soil.

THOMAS MERTON

Oneness

All things love one another. Everything in nature feels fellow with all the rest. All living beings are in communion with each other. All plants, animals and things have family features and copy one another. There are insects which imitate flowers and flowers which imitate insects, animals which are like water, rocks, the sand of the desert, snow, trees or other animals. All living beings love one another (and eat one another) and they are all joined in the vast process of birth, growth, reproduction and death. All things in nature are mutation, transformation and change, of the one into the other; they hug and caress and kiss. And like the laws governing living things, the laws governing inert nature (which is also alive with a life we cannot see) are all contained in the one law of love. All physical phenomena are the one phenomenon of love. The condensation of the snowflake is one with the explosion of a new star, a nova. The beetle clinging to its dung-dropping is one with the lover clinging to his love. Everything in nature tries to break down its own limits and go beyond the confines of its individuality, seeking someone to whom to give itself, into whom to transform itself. The laws of thermodynamics and electrodynamics, the laws of light and universal gravity are all one and the same law of love. Everything in nature is incomplete, offers itself to another and clasps that other to it.

All beings in their most secret self and deepest depth are hunger and thirst for love.

Things are related to one another, one is contained in another and that other in others still, so that the whole universe is one immense being.

The whole of nature touches and intertwines. The whole of nature embraces. The wind brushing me, the sun kissing me, the air that I breathe, the fish swimming in the water, the far-off star and I who look up at it are all in contact. What we call the empty space between the stars is made of the same matter as the stars, except that it is thinner and more rarefied. The stars are merely a denser concentration of this interstellar matter, and the whole universe is like one big star. We all share in this universe through one and the same rhythm, the rhythm of universal gravity, which is the force binding chaotic matter, joining molecules, bringing particles of matter together at any particular point in the universe, causing the stars to be stars. This is the rhythm of love.

We are all in contact and we are all incomplete. And this incomplete nature strains towards its own perfection. This is called evolution. The most perfect thing in nature is mankind. We also are incomplete. We too are imperfect and strain towards another, towards God. And when we love God, we love him with the urgency of all nature, the groaning of the creatures and all the desire in all evolution. The whole of creation groans with us, as Paul says, as if it were in labour. It is the pain of the mighty process of evolution.

When monks sing in choir they are singing in the name of all creation, for everything in nature from the electron to men and women, is a single psalm. We cannot rest till we find God. Only he can satisfy our heart and the enormous love that is in us with all the force of universal gravity. Towards him all creatures strain.

And all things speak to us of God, because all things long for him, the starry sky and all insects, the huge galaxies and the chipmunk playing all day long, startled by anything that comes near it and hiding from it (its every movement is an unconscious movement towards God).

All stars move towards him and the expansion of the universe is towards him. All stars and the primeval gas itself came from him, and only in him can the universe find rest.

Thirst

The prairie wolf howling in the night howls for God and the owl hoots for him. The gentle dove moans for him and does not know it. The little calf mooing for his mother is also calling God, as is the lion's roar and the croaking of frogs. All creation calls him, in all its many languages. And lovers' and poets' language and the prayer of monks also cry to God.

All human eyes have longing in them. People of all races, children, the old, mothers, women in love, policemen, workers, adventurers, murderers, revolutionaries, dictators and saints all have the same light of longing, the same deep fire, the same infinite desire for happiness and joy without end. Human eyes are like wells, like the well of the Samaritan woman.

Every woman is a woman at the well. The well is deep. And Jesus is sitting on the rim of the well.

'And the woman said to him, "Sir, you have nothing to draw with and the well is deep . . ."

'Jesus said to her, "Every one who drinks of this water will thirst again, but whoever drinks of the water that I shall give him will never thirst; the water that I shall give him will become in him a spring of water welling up to eternal life." '

'The woman said to him, "Sir, give me this water that I may not thirst." '

This thirst felt by all beings is the love of God.

For this love's sake, all crimes are committed, all wars are fought and all men love or hate each other. For this love's sake men climb mountains, go down to the ocean bed; they rule and plot and build and write and sing and cry and love. Every human action, even sin, is a search for God. But sometimes he is sought where he cannot be found. Thus Augustine: 'Seek what you seek but not where you seek it.' For what we seek in orgies, at parties, on journeys, in cinemas and bars is simply God. He is only to be found within ourselves.

Within every one of us there is the same cry and the same thirst: 'As pants the hart for cooling streams, so longs my soul, O God, for thee,' says the psalm. His arrow has pierced every heart.

The dictator's lust for power, money and property is the love of God. The lover finding his way to his love's house, the explorer, the businessman, the agitator, the artist and the contemplative monk are all looking for the same thing: heaven.

Girls' faces are a reflection of heaven and that is why they so attract us, for we were created for heaven.

God is everyone's home. For him alone we are homesick. In every creature God calls us, his call is the charm of the creature. We hear his call deep within us, as the lark hears its mate calling at daybreak, or Juliet hears Romeo whispering under her balcony.

Evening and night are quiet and solitary because God made them for contemplation. Woods, deserts, the sea and the starry sky were made for contemplation. For it all the world was made.

Magpies and coal-tits speak of God; he taught them to speak. The bird chorus in the early morning sings to God. Volcanoes, clouds and trees shout about God. All creation cries out with a loud voice that God is, is beautiful and loves. Music sings in our ears and beautiful countryside tells our eyes.

'I find letters from God dropped in the street and they are all signed by him,' says Whitman. And the green grass is a fragrant handkerchief with God's initials on the corner; as Whitman says, he dropped it on purpose to remind us of him. That is how the saints see nature, and how Adam saw it in Eden (and poets and artists see it like this in some measure, some of the time).

God's signature is on the whole of nature. All creatures are love letters from God to us. They are outbursts of love. The whole of nature is bursting with love, set in it by God, who is love, to kindle the fire of love in us. All things have no other reason for existing, no other meaning. They can give us no satisfaction or pleasure beyond this, to stir in us the love of God.

Nature is like God's shadow, reflecting his beauty and splendour. The quiet blue lake has the splendour of God. His finger-prints are upon every particle of matter. The image of the Trinity is in every atom, the figure of God the three in one. That is why God's creation is so disturbing.

And my body was also made for the love of God. Every cell in my body is a hymn to my creator and a declaration of love.

As the kingfisher was made to fish and the humming

bird to suck nectar from flowers, we were made for contemplation and to love God.

God is everywhere, not just within us. But he is also within us and we have felt his presence and want it and that is why we withdraw into silence and solitude. For the time being we want no other creature to impress us, only God. As the lake reflects the sky when it is calm, we find God's reflection best in solitude and peace. We have only to be quiet and purified for God's face to show. And God's face is the Son of Man, whose face was printed on Veronica's veil. And his face also shows, but less clearly, in all creation.

We are mirrors of God, created to reflect him. Even when the water is not calm, it reflects the sky.

Initials

All nature speaks and sings and is musical. All things whisper, sigh, moan, warble, whistle, bellow, howl, roar, wail, shriek, cry or complain. The voice of the grasshopper, cricket and frog, the chatter of chipmunks calling each other, and all animal sounds are a prayer. So is the human voice. That is why contemplative monks are silent. They have dedicated their voices to sing only in choir, because they have understood that the voice is a prayer.

All nature is made up of symbols which speak to us of God. Creation is in his handwriting, in which every sign makes sense. The path of meteors in the sky and the trail of molluscs on the sand, the formations of migrating birds on autumn evenings, the sun's course through the zodiac and the circles in the trunk of the cedar tree marking the springs and the winters, the lightning's jagged edge and the winding of rivers in photographs taken from the air, all are signs with a message for those who can read. People who are moved by looking at these signs but do not understand them, because they do not know that all nature is written for them, are like the country girl who enjoys looking at the beautiful writing on a letter which has come into her hands but, because she cannot read, does not know that these signs are a love letter from the emperor to her.

We too are signs of God. Each one of us bears his handwriting, and our whole being is a message from God. We have been written into creation, which all speaks of God, as the particularly important words. We are in the image of God.

We have made gods in our own image and likeness because God first made us in his image and likeness.

The reason why human love exists is that the human face is the image and likeness of God's. We love God in the faces of our fellow men. Every human face is veiled. It is his veil whom we cannot see face to face and live.

We were created for a *plural* God, God who spoke in the plural when he created man: 'Let us make man in our own image and likeness.' Every one of us bears the image of this plurality, the Holy Trinity. That is to say, the image of love. For God is love (between persons) and we were created in the image of a social God.

This image of God in us is the face of Christ. The face of Christ is printed on our faces as it was on Veronica's veil. This face is printed on every lovely thing, on the face of every beautiful woman. St John Climaco tells the story of a man who burned with love of God whenever he saw a beautiful woman, and burst into tears, praising God.

The Jewish people were forbidden to make images of God because man (Christ) is the image of God. And even animals are God's image because they are the image of men who are the image of God (and that's why we love animals).

God's image was blurred by sin (devils are faces which have lost God's image), but with Christ it was reprinted on man. With Christ we become again the the image and word of God, for he is the word and the image of the Father ('he who has seen me has seen the Father').

The word of God is only revealed to us in silence.

It is in the depths of every being and deep within us too. We do not have to go far to find it, we do not have to go out of ourselves. We do not have to go far to find happiness, we have only to find ourselves. We have only to go deep down into ourselves and find our own identity (which is in God). People nowadays are always trying to get away from themselves. They are unable to be silent or alone, because then they would be by themselves. So places of entertainment like cinemas are always full. And if they sometimes are alone and about to meet God, they turn on the radio or the television.

Image of God

Prayer is as natural to us as speaking, sighing or gazing, or the beating heart of the lover. Prayer *is* complaining and sighing and gazing and the quickened heartbeat. It is natural to us, an instinct, but since we are fallen we must relearn it, because it has become a forgotten instinct.

Prayer is establishing contact with God. It is a communication with God and it does not have to be in words or even with the mind. We can communicate by a look, a smile, a sigh or a gesture. Smoking can be a prayer, or painting a picture or looking up at the sky or drinking water. All our bodily actions are prayers. Our body gives grateful thanks when it is thirsty and drinks a glass of water, or when we plunge into a cool river on a hot day; our very being sings a hymn of thanksgiving to our creator. We may not have thought about this prayer or intended it, it may even be in spite of us. But we can turn everything we do into a prayer. Work is an existential prayer. The Lord told Angela de Foligno that he was pleased with all her actions, even her eating and drinking and sleeping. He was pleased with her whole being, even her bodily functions.

The *Little Flowers* tell us that Brother Maseo's prayer was simply repeating 'Ooh, ooh, ooh!' And that Brother Bernard's prayer was running over the mountain.

God enfolds us like an atmosphere. Just as the atmosphere is full of sight and sound waves which we cannot see or hear except through the proper channels, so we are surrounded by the waves of God which we cannot pick up except through the proper channels. We cannot pick up God's waves if we live in this world purely through our senses.

We can communicate with one another through God, as if by telecommunication through the atmosphere, just as two friends or lovers can communicate even though they are far apart in distant cities. And they can be closer together in spite of the distance, than two neighbours who are only separated by a party wall in the same village.

But God is also infinitely far from us. We are infinitely distant from him. Union with God is like lovers kissing through a pane of glass.

We see God darkly. He is like a film we can't see on the screen until the doors are shut and the lights out. As the room grows darker, the picture on the screen becomes clearer. Or he is like a house in which all the lights are out except in one inner room, and you grope through the rooms and along the dark corridors, bumping into the furniture, as you are led by the hand to the lighted room by someone who knows the house.

God's presence is also elusive and veiled. And it becomes more so as God comes nearer. It is like a very delicate form of lens, between our sight and reality. We must not use force on it to try to break it. We are so near him that we cannot see him.

We do not feel the presence of God because we are used to experience coming to us from the outside and this experience comes from within. We are turned outwards, de-

pendent on outward sensation, and we do not notice what
is going on inside us.

We think that if God spoke to us it would be with a
physical voice that would strike our ears from without.

Or we believe that God's presence is simply ourselves,
and we do not recognize him. We do not know that at the
centre of our being we find not ourselves but another, that
our identity is in another, that turning inwards and finding
ourselves is to fall into the arms of another.

We are always seeking his embrace, but in the wrong
way, by turning outwards. We hear him calling us within
and we think he is whispering outside.

God is everywhere, even on Broadway, but we can only
hear his voice in silence.

Identity

For St Teresa, life was a night spent in an uncomfortable inn, just as for Cervantes the castles of human illusions were really humble inns. But for St Teresa the soul is a castle, like the castles on the plain of Castile. And the centre of our being, where God is, is the marriage bed in the castle. For most people it is the dungeon which they never go down to. But it is really the secret room, the bridal chamber in each one of us.

Love dwells within us. God is crazed with love and his behaviour is therefore unpredictable. He may do something silly at any time, because, like the lover, he does not reason. He is drunk with love.

The soul is the secret chamber for which only God has the key. And if he does not go in, it is empty. The senses may be surfeited with pleasure but the soul remains empty.

I saw Venice and Capri and I was delighted by their beauty but I was not satisfied. Something was lacking. The dregs of every pleasure were melancholy and anguish. And now my memories are as unreal as picture postcards. It was an empty vision.

All beauty is sad. Bitterness and distress are in the depths of all things. This is the groaning of the creatures, of which St Paul speaks. But in us creation rests from its anguish, when our hearts rest in God.

We tire of the cinema and parties and yachts. But we do not tire of God. Trappists do not need recreation for their whole life is a recreation. Likewise birds and squirrels do not need playtime, for their whole life, even when they are at work looking for food, is recreation and permanent playtime.

And what would an oil magnate or a steel magnate give to buy this peace. If he knew about it he would give his whole empire. Just as anyone who has ever known about it has given all his possessions. For millionaires seek happiness in money, and any millionaire would give all his money if he knew where happiness was to be found. (Monks and nuns are people who have given all they had, or all they might have had, for this happiness.)

How many boys and girls, at this moment at parties, the cinema, in bars or nightclubs have been called by God to a life of contemplation? Perhaps he has kept the highest mystical gifts for them and they do not know it and may never know it in this life.

Many people grasp the pleasures of the senses with mystical fervour. They are seeking God where he cannot be found, and when they do not find him they become desperate. They may turn to vice or crime, go mad or commit suicide. They seek happiness in money, in women, in wine, in night clubs. They seek it with all the strength of their faculties created for the beatific vision.

Love of loves

The girl who dreams most of love, who is burning with love or the desire for love, she who most craves life and romance is the one who has the greatest capacity for surrendering herself to Jesus. She seeks him in her dreams, at dances and in all her loving but she does not find him there.

We were created for love, for a God who is love. And the worst sufferings and the hardest pains of each one of us are caused by love. How many people live a boring and sterile life in this world, loveless, looking for a love to fill them but never finding it. Or suffering the bitterness of disappointed love. Or the anguish of impossible, lost or forbidden love and not finding fulfilment. Or the sadness of love returned which does not satisfy. These people could be overwhelmed with love and their almost limitless capacity for love, tenderness and self-surrender could be filled, if they would only turn inwards to the inexhaustible love which lives and breathes within them. Their lives would be rapturous, they would smile and sigh and take delight in a paradise of love. But their lives are without love, they feel that time passes, spring follows spring, they grow old and love does not come. And perhaps spring will come yet again and love still not come.

Passion

God is love. And we are also love because we are made in his image and likeness.

God is love and as he is infinitely simple, if he is love he must be nothing but love. If he is infinite good, infinite wisdom, infinite truth, infinite beauty and infinite justice, this simply means that he is love which is infinitely good, infinitely wise, infinitely true, infinitely beautiful and infinitely just. But he is love alone.

And we who are made in God's image are also love alone. Our rational being is one sole desire, one sole passion, the thirst and the cry for love.

Whatever has not been falsified in us is love. Ontologically we are love. And God like us is a cry of love, an infinite passion and infinite thirst for love. Love is our reason for existing.

And this love of God and our own love are the same love, and it has no end, like the fire of hell. It is a thirst which can never be quenched because the more we drink the more we desire.

And in our being and in all our movements we keep the memory of God from whom we came, even when we are far from him. We are like sea creatures who keep the memory of the sea even when they have been put in a laboratory, and they still go on moving with the rhythm of the waves even though the sea is very far off.

The Father knows no rest until creation returns to him, like the prodigal son. He longs for us with infinite yearning and the Holy Spirit is the sigh of this longing.

The word of God was made man for love of us and for love of the Father, to love the Father in us and for God to love God in millions of souls and millions of lives.

We are love's invention and we were created to love. We are high-tension wires carrying the power of love. We should not therefore fall into self-love, because self-love cuts us off. We should love others as we love ourselves, because loving ourselves most interferes with love. We should surrender ourselves totally to love and let its power run through us. We should be transmitters of love.

Every created being is in communion with God's being, but in non-rational beings this communion is more imperfect and limited. We are the only creatures in the whole universe capable of love. We are born with aching hearts, as the heart of Jesus was also pierced. We are not a meaningless passion, as Sartre calls us, but a passion whose meaning is God.

Me

Holiness is our true personality. No two leaves are the same and no two people. But sin levels us and makes us uniform. The saints however are all different. They have found the identity which each of us has but has lost through sin.

The more we identify with God, the more we become ourselves. The closer our identification with God, the clearer our own identity, not because our essence is God, but because our essence is to be the image of God, which is nearly the same thing.

The more like God we are, the more we are ourselves. Our destiny is to be a portrait—self-portrait—of God. We are not infinite but we are an image of the infinite, which is nearly the same thing.

We do not know how beautiful the human soul is because we have never seen it. But we have seen the absence of the soul, the corruption of the body when the soul has left it. The rotting body can give us an idea in reverse of what the soul is. The beauty of the living body, whose soul is in it, can give us an idea of what the beauty of the soul might be without the body. And great works of art reflect the soul of the artist. We glimpse something when we draw near the mystery of another human soul in friendship or in love.

God's love and beauty gives the soul its beauty and the

soul which mirrors God is glowing with love. An infinite beauty and an infinite love are reflected in it like the deep blue sky in Lake Nicaragua in May.

The disembodied soul is all smiles and emotion and love, trembling and passion and fire, pure tenderness and feeling, pure vitality and pure life. And when it is united to God, the more it gazes at him the better it knows him and the better it knows him the more it loves him, and the more it loves him the more it possesses and knows and loves him, and its whole life is giving and receiving, enjoying and loving more and more and trembling with love.

The soul is passive to God and feminine. It cannot take the initiative. It cannot visit God because it does not know how to get to him, or where he is. It must wait for him to come and if he does not come, it remains alone. It cannot move from where it is. God comes and goes, visits and leaves. Neither does the soul know how to caress. It only sometimes very timidly caresses God. But it knows how to let God caress it and this is all it knows. It does not know how to kiss God. He kisses it tenderly or passionately. The soul lets itself be kissed and faints with love.

The soul of an old woman is as tender and young and fresh as a child's, because it is the source of life and does not grow old as times passes. And the soul of the grossest of men is as full of light as the soul of Beethoven or Dante. And the souls of men are as feminine as the souls of women. The soul is the principle of life. It is pure innocence, pure light and joy and lightness and sweetness and grace. And that is why God is so in love with it. Everyone walking in the street has a soul like this. And it is so sad that this soul gives itself to such inferior loves and is enslaved by food and drink, games and money.

Occasionally we glimpse the beauty of the soul in pure eyes, through which the soul shines palely as through opaque material, as the sun sometimes shines through closed eyelids.

But soul and body are the same thing while the body is alive. The soul is the life and vitality of the body and prevents it becoming a corpse. 'If the body is not the soul, what is the soul?' Whitman asked. As Aristotle said, the soul is the substance which gives the body its form.

God's reflection in opaque matter dazzles us. His reflection is the splendour of all beautiful material things. How much more shall his beauty dazzle us when it is not reflected in opaque matter but in a pure spirit which is like God. The essence of all natural beauties, the common denominator of all the beautiful (in the blue sea and lakes and snowy mountains and deserts, women, flowers and stars) is also in the human soul but in a more concentrated way, as if it had evolved further, refined and transformed into a higher beauty which is pure spirit like God; as if many lovely smiles and beautiful landscapes were all combined; and yet more.

'We are not hollow inside, daughters,' says St Teresa.

Centre

God does not love us as a group. He loves us individually.

The mere fact that we exist proves his infinite and eternal love, for from all eternity he chose us from among an infinite number of possible beings. He chose us, not those other possible beings and so they did not exist. And among all these others he also chose you, individually. He chose you from an infinity of possible beings who could have existed but which he did not create. You were the one chosen from an infinite number of possibilities and the very fact that you exist is the greatest proof of God's preference for you.

Each of us is irreplaceable. We are all unique collector's pieces because God is an artist who never repeats or reproduces himself. No two leaves are alike, no two finger-prints are alike, even less are any two souls alike. The soul that is lost God does not reproduce for all eternity and he feels the loss forever.

God loves us more than we love ourselves. He loves us as only God can love, as he loves himself. How bitter will be his disappointment if he is eternally separated from any one of us.

God is love. And his love is despised. This is bitter for him. Sometimes we see him as a tyrant demanding more and more, but he is simply love beseeching. The creator of the universe begs for your love.

God loves each one of us as if there were only the two of us in the whole universe. God does not need humans in order to be happy, but he loves us as if he would be eternally unhappy without us. Although he has lived from all eternity without needing human beings, he humiliates and enslaves himself for love of us, as if he could not live without us. God loves the human soul so much, says St Catherine of Genoa, that it is as if God were a slave and the soul God.

Sometimes it seems as if God has forgotten all the rest of the universe and wants only to talk to a single soul.

Like a lover who spends all his time thinking of his love far away, God has been thinking of me since before I was born, for all eternity.

And we also long for God, we are homesick for him from the time we are born. Life for us is exile from God. God is love and we who are made in his image, are also love. Every cell in our body is love, made for love, as the grain of incense is made for the fire. And our whole being is ready to burn in this fire.

The one thing that separates us from God is selfishness, self-love. So our union with God can only be through the death of self. Either God or me. As soon as our self surrenders within us, God comes in.

We have only to repeat Mary's *fiat*, for God to be incarnate again in us. A transubstantiation takes place in us as in the bread and wine, and our flesh and blood are changed into Christ, the flesh and blood of God. We become a eucharist, a sacrifice of love.

For St Bernard mystical union is a mutual exchange.

God becomes the soul and the soul becomes God. Love always makes two things one. Here on earth two beings never become completely one. Only God becomes one with the soul, without ceasing to be himself.

Nature

God is love. And is there any greater joy than love, than loving and being loved? God is joy because he is love, because he is the joy of love. He is the infinite joy of infinite love.

And everything that exists sprang from this love. All things were made by love and all things are love.

God would not have created a thing had he hated it, as the Book of Wisdom says (11.24–5), and the mere fact that he keeps it in being is the proof that he loves it. The existence of all things is the love of God, his loving kiss.

Picasso was right when he said that we do not know what a tree or a window is. All things are very mysterious and strange (Picassian) and we only overlook their strangeness and their mystery because we are so used to them. We only understand things very obscurely. But what are things? Things are God's love become things.

God also communicates with us through all things. Things are messages of love. When I read a book, God is speaking to me through this book. I raise my eyes to look at the countryside: God created it for me to see. The picture I look at today was inspired by God in the painter, for me to see. Everything I enjoy was given lovingly by God for me to enjoy and all my pain was also given to me by God for me to enjoy and all my pain was also given to me by God lovingly.

God's love created the world and continues creating it at every moment through the process of evolution. Because God the creator is also master of evolution, the world's evolution is the work of his love. When God said 'Increase and multiply', he gave the law of evolution.

The world is not like a picture painted by an artist centuries ago which now hangs untouchable in a museum. It is more like a work of art in constant process of creation, still in the studio.

God is not made of marble, as Paul told the Athenians on the Areopagus when he saw their marble sculptures. God is not sculpture at all. He is the living God and in him 'we live and move and have our being'. From him came the marble on the Areopagus and the hand that worked the marble and the inspiration which moved the hand.

Each of us makes himself the centre of the universe and therefore lives in a false universe, like the astronomers' universe before Copernicus. Things interest us to the extent that they serve our own small interests. But we can only be happy if God is the centre of our universe. Then we will be glad about everything that exists and that things are as they are and happen as they happen. For God wants it so whether or not it is convenient to our own little notions.

God is love but our self-love is anti-love for love is self-surrender and self-love is giving way to self or not giving ourself to another. Self-love is the opposite of love. It is love turned inwards, it is hate.

We find it difficult to love others as we love ourselves. Difficult to do or even to think of. But this will be our natural state in heaven, because this *is* our natural state.

Mankind was created as an organic whole, even though it is made up of individuals. 'So God created man in his own image, in the image of God he created him; male and female he created them.' (Gen. 1.27). Mankind is a single body comprising many individuals. Individual self-love is unnatural, as is the self-love of one cell in our own body. When one cell puts itself first and before the organic functioning of the whole body, when it declares war on the other cells, this is cancer. Self-love is the cancer of the whole mystical body. Or, as Paul says, 'The eye cannot say to the hand, "I have no need of you," nor again the head to the feet, "I have no need of you."' (1 Cor. 12.21.)

Longing

All nature is *charity* but only the mystic experiences this love completely. The love of God surrounds us. His love is the water we drink, the air we breathe and the light we see. All natural phenomena are different material forms of the love of God. We move in his love as the fish in the water. And we are so close to him, so wrapped in his love and showered with his gifts (we ourselves are his gift) that we do not realize it for lack of perspective. His love surrounds us but we do not feel it any more than we feel the pressure of the atmosphere.

Nature is God's love made perceptible to the senses, materialized. His providence is visible in all we see. Men hurry through the streets preoccupied and never stop for a moment to think of God, or to remember that in him they move, that he surrounds them and that every hair of their head is counted, every cell in their body is counted. Why are we so preoccupied?

Why do men go through cities frowning and preoccupied, as if each were alone in a strange and hostile world? Why do we fuss about what we eat and drink and wear and what brand we should buy. Consider the birds of the air and lilies of the field. Consider the sea anemone and the humble protozoan, they neither sow nor reap, they have neither barns nor bank accounts nor life insurance.

God has taken care of the earth by his providence for billions of years but you feel strange and lonely in the universe, preoccupied with your affairs as if there were no one to take care of you. You forget that someone is taking care of every fibre of your being at every moment, governing the flow of your blood and the functioning of your glands. And you believe there is no one but you in the whole universe who can solve a small problem in your practical life.

He hears the voice of the stag in the valley, calling for a mate and he gives him one. He cares for the cuckoo demanding food. He guides the swans in their migrations. When the weasel and the badger sleep in the early morning, he watches for them. The little frog, the beetle and the raven all find food in due time every day.

> 'These all look to thee,
> to give them their food in due season.
> When thou givest to them, they gather it up;
> when thou openest thy hand, they are filled with good
>   things.'

(Ps. 104. 27-8.)

God & nothing

Every human being is born with love in his heart, he is born thirsty. 'My soul thirsts for thee like a parched land' (Ps. 143). God created eating and drinking as material symbols of this love.

This thirst for God is the anxiety on all the faces of all the people walking in the street, going into shops, cinemas and bars. Everyone wants things, many things, an infinity of things: one more glass, one more sweet, one more look, one more word, one more kiss, one more book, one more journey. Always more and more and more. Human faces are racked with anxiety and desire. We who have escaped from this slavery are like escaped prisoners remembering the Nazi concentration camps or forced labour in Siberia.

A man thinks just a little more will do, then he wants still more. He thinks he could be content with a small house and a car, a lovely wife and children. But he always goes out into the street with the same anxious face. He goes on seeking new things with the same eagerness. He buys a newspaper in the street with the same eagerness, throws it away in the street and remains always unsatisfied. The desire for possession is like an incurable disease.

As Plato says, the human body is a cracked vase which cannot be filled. The senses may be surfeited with pleasures but the soul remains unsatisfied. The body's pleasures have

not reached it and have only made its mouth water, and feel
that the cup that cheers has not yet touched its lips.

It is like trying to satisfy ourselves with food that does
not fill us or wine that does not warm us. Food fills us and
wine excites us but they do not satisfy our deepest need.
They make us feel it but do nothing for it. We can be
surfeited with food and wine but they do not satisfy.

And just as we realize how deep a well must be when we
throw a stone in and do not hear it fall, we realize how
deep our soul must be when things drop into it and disappear without us hearing them hit the bottom.

Because God is in the depths of every soul, its depths are
infinite and nothing can fill them but God. A wine to
satisfy would have to be infinite. Only the water that Christ
offered the Samaritan woman by the well can satisfy. It is
such a wine.

But in monasteries we see men who are fulfilled and content. They smile and do not have anxious frowns on their
faces. Ignatius of Loyola said that if he was forced to dis-
solve his Society, he would regain his inner peace in fifteen
minutes.

Animals are also peaceful. They do not go about an-
xiously, but are quiet and content like monks.

Human beings are never satisfied with earthly things because they were not created for earthly things. Animals satisfy their needs and want nothing more. They do not thirst
for the infinite. This earth is their heaven. So animals are
not disappointed by life and never commit suicide, because
they were created for this earth. (Thus all animals are saints
with an animal sanctity; they are chaste, poor and obedient
like monks, and humble.)

But our whole being is designed to love God and to be

with him and enjoy him, just as the mackerel's body is made to swim through the water and the seagull's to fly over the sea.

Just as a telephone is designed for telephonic conversation and not for anything else, human beings were not made to enjoy this life but to enjoy God and to love God and so can only be happy with God.

And although we have not seen God, we are like migrating birds or fishes, who were born in a strange place but when winter comes feel a mysterious restlessness in the blood, a longing for another warmer country which they have never seen. They set out for it without knowing where it is. They have felt the call of the promised land. They hear a beloved voice calling: 'Arise, my love, my fair one and come away; for lo the winter is past, the rain is over and gone.' (Song of Songs 2.10.)

The human soul is born loving. But it does not see the one it loves. He is reflected in all created things and so we cling to them. The infant eagerly stretches out its tiny arms towards everything it sees, and tries to put everything it touches in its mouth, and wants to touch and pick up everything. Later on it clings to its toys and even grown up continues to cling to things. But we are never satisfied because what we cling to is not God, unless one day we leave hold of things and turn to God.

But God can only be found in *nothingness*. He is where no things are.

Things cannot be possessed and leave us always unsatisfied. 'O world I cannot embrace enough!' exclaims the poet Edna St Vincent Millay, who wrote such a lot about embracing. This is the pain of the human heart. It longs to possess the world but it cannot. (Alexander wept because he could not conquer the stars.) And we want to possess another human body in love but we cannot. Only God can be totally possessed. We can only embrace God, because our arms were made to embrace the infinite and nothing less.

We can embrace neither world nor women, they cannot embrace us. Neither world nor women satisfy. Only God satisfies.

God gives us the joy of pleasure and the headiness of wine without our drinking. He is all pleasures and joys and delights, and all love, infinitely, not like the shadows of pleasure and joy and delight and the shadows of love which we pursue.

In him is the beauty of all women, the taste of all fruit, the power of all wine and the sweetness and bitterness of all loves on earth. To taste one drop of God turns our head forever.

Someone who has tasted one drop of this blessedness cannot go on living as he did before, going to the office every morning and keeping up the conventions. He goes mad and breaks all the rules. He may walk the street in rags or wearing a dunce's cap so that people laugh at him. He may preach in the streets or shut himself up in a cell for the rest of his life. He may kiss lepers. People call it a 'conversion'.

Loving God is now my one reason for living, my only profession, my only office. I have surrendered to him as passionately as I used to surrender to female beauty and I have given myself to him as I once gave myself to women, wholly and completely. And I know that he will love me and satisfy me as they never did. And I know I will find in him the well remembered shapes of all those beautiful faces I once loved. I love him with the love I had for all his handiwork, particularly the love I had for women, the most beautiful of all his creations. I used to love them as passionately and violently as I now love God, with love that should have been for God. My love has remained but its object is not the same. The burning thirst, the desert heat, the almost cosmic hunger for love, the insatiable longing, the empty heart remain. All my former loves have died. Now I love only God, with all my love. Lord have pity on my empty heart.

Infinity

God is love. But love is always love of something or someone. God is love of what? Love of God, naturally. But love of God, who is love, is love of love. Love of a love which is also love of love and so on, infinitely. This is why God is infinite. Infinite love of infinite love or an infinite mutuality of love.

God is *mutual*. He is one and also two, two in one and this mutual union of the two is also God and so God is also three and one. Love of love, God is love loving itself as a mirror reflected in another mirror, making an infinite number of mirrors of an infinite mirror.

God is three because he is love, an infinite projection procreation and transmission of himself and giving in love. He is one because he is love, unity, identification and communion of the lover and the beloved embracing in love.

And loving God is sharing in God, because God is this love of himself. But God's love is not selfishness but surrender, God is not self love but mutual love, because God is mutual, because God is love.

And loving others is also sharing in God. What we love in others is what is godlike in them. And we love them with what is godlike in us. And what others love in us is what we have of God in us. So all mutual love is the mutual love of the godlike.

People who love each other give each other a gift which is the very substance of God. If God were unity alone, he would be all alone, begetting nothing, and so a loveless and sterile God. But he is unity in distinctness. All that is distinct, all plurality in creation comes from him. As does all the individuality and unity in all things. Our union of one with another is an image of his union. And our union of all with Christ is a sharing in the union of the trinity.

God's love of himself is not selfish; it is the love of one person for another, for an infinite other. And there is an infinite distinction between the two persons and the love between them is another infinite person who is also God.

And the Son loves the Father through us as if we were an electric cable. When there is no selfishness in us he loves God through us with a love that is God, that is the Holy Spirit, 'the Spirit of our Lord Jesus Christ', as Paul says.

The Holy Spirit is the love of the Father and Son, inspiration and breath and kiss. The Son is the word of God and the Holy Spirit is God's sighing and groaning, the sound of his love. The Son is the projection and expression of God, God's conversation, and the Holy Spirit is the sighing of two who love one another.

This is the dogma of love, the dogma of the Holy Trinity. The mystery that God is not alone, that God is union, communion and communism.

St Ignatius was moved to tears in the streets of Rome whenever he saw three of anything: three pigeons, three men, three stars in the sky, three children playing, because they reminded him of this mystery of the Trinity. The Trinity is love. Every human family with a father, mother and child is an image of the Trinity, as is all natural fertility, for in nature too everything is trinity and all things come from other things and each thing joins with another making two and a third is born of this union.

God is three and one, but his number is not that of our counting 1,2,3,4. He is an infinite one and an infinite three and in him all number and all unity are contained.

God is above number, as his name (the word) is above every other name, for every other word and every other name stands for or symbolizes something. The infinite word not only stands for or symbolizes but is the thing itself, which is infinite. It is the infinite name of an infinite reality and the name is the reality. When God told his name he said 'he who is', that is, he whose existence is his name. Or he who has no name but simply exists. Or he whose name is existence. And this is the name the Father gave his Son, 'a name which is above every other name', as Paul says, above our semantics and beyond all language. 'This glorious and awful name the LORD your God' (Deuteronomy 28.58).

Light & darkness

The atheist who denies the existence of God is also partly proclaiming a truth about God: God's non-existence in the sense that other things exist, or what the theologians call his 'transcendence'. Denis the Areopagite, Master Eckhardt and Suso and other mystics also call God the Nothing, the Great Nothing. For God is no-thing as other things are, he is Nothing in comparison with things. He is a non-being. If we call what all things have existence, God does not exist. And if we call what God is existence, then nothing else exists. He is simply so different from everything that it is as if he did not exist. Or if he exists, everything else is nothing in his sight. So in a certain sense God does not exist, and in a certain sense he alone exists.

And the atheists are also right, in a certain sense, to deny God. For by God they mean an anthropomorphic God, a God who does not exist, a fairytale God. But when they feel the existence of something vague and incomprehensible and mysterious and they themselves do not know what it is or what it is called, but they will not call it God or give it any attribute of God, then they are also darkly affirming the existence of God, a being they can neither understand nor imagine, that no man can look upon and live. Their God is also the Unknown God of the Areopagus in Athens. Paul told the atheists that the unknown one was the true God whom they worshipped without knowing.

God is not only light but darkness. The idea of 'nothing-ness' that atheists have of God is the same nothingness that the mystics knew by *experience*. They had personal experience of this nothingness, they had proved its bottomless abyss of sweetness and love, they had felt its caress and kiss.

God is light and darkness together, or better, he is neither light nor darkness, but when he created the world he separated the light from the darkness for us, and made us 'sons of light'. We cannot have the knowledge of good and evil, but only the knowledge of good, and we were created in light, together with everything else. God alone has the knowledge of good and evil. Mystical experience is experience of this darkness in God, or of God's reality where there is no separation of light and darkness, from which both day and night came. For God is also the creator of night. He is also night. Night of love and mystery. And we who came from it also long for this night.

God is infinitely beautiful but we could also say that there is an 'ugliness' in God, not beauty alone. For his beauty is beyond all our ideas of beauty. 'To create something new you always have to make it ugly', Picasso said. And God is infinite newness. We know the invisible perfections of God through the visible world, Paul said. The fascinating beauty of certain reptiles and insects, monsters of the deep and weird creatures of the microcosmos (and also modern art) suggests something of what the terrible, eternally new and revolutionary beauty of God might be.

And God also has a sense of humour, an infinite one. We know his invisible perfections through the visible world; the green lizard, the rabbit, the locust, the protozoan, the praying mantis, kneeling on its outsize knees as if it were in prayer, suggest something about God's sense of humour.

And God is not only infinitely great, but as Denis the Areopagite says, 'God is also small'. He is infinitely small. And just as we get a conception of the infinite greatness of God by looking at the macrocosm through a telescope, we can also discover God's infinite littleness by looking at the microcosm through a microscope. And if the starry sky or the sea proclaim the grandeur of God, insects' eyes and the ant's digestive system proclaim God's lowliness. For if we can say that God is greater than the whole universe, we can also say that God is smaller than an electron.

'Everything you say of him is false,' says Master Eckhardt.

Looking

Sometimes we feel God looking at us intently, infinitely, with an infinite intensity fixed from all eternity. At other times we feel we are looking at God, opening wide the eyes of our soul, our whole self in our gaze, our whole soul in our gaze, and our gaze and his gaze meet and come together, as if he were in our eyes, the lover and the beloved together. At other times the little soul feels God embracing her or feels herself embracing him. Sometimes she clutches at air but at others feels a sure contact with God. Sometimes it is the gentlest of caresses ruffling the soul and the skin with a delicious excitement (for 'if the soul is not the body, what is the soul?'). Sometimes our whole self yearns, we become pure longing, loving with each heart beat and each breath, with every cell and gland and organ, pulsing with a love that goes up and down, up and down.

The soul is feminine, and sometimes a little coquettish in the presence of God. She knows she is loved and can charm and master him. Sometimes she is even a bit tyrannical, knowing that he has surrendered to her and she has power over him, but also knowing that she too has surrendered and is in his power.

And at night she sleeps smiling and confident, knowing that she is loved and cherished by her beloved. Sometimes she wakes in the night feeling that he has kissed her and that his face is near her own, the face on Veronica's veil.

Today I looked at you for a long time with sad and tearful eyes, the hungry eyes of my soul, you the source of the beauty and grace of women, of Maria, Claudia, Sylvia and Miriam and all the others, creator of their hair and eyes, their smiles and dresses, and of all the beauties in the world, which are reflections of your beauty, and of all the loves in the world which are reflections of your love, the light in the eyes of the lover when he sees his love, the love of two birds together, the love of all people and all animals. We are alone in the chapel you and I. Outside the world's traffic passes and at these moments I have nothing and no one. I am totally dispossessed and alone in the world. But I have everything, I am happy, I lack nothing, want nothing. Because what others seek in a woman or a family, in friends, at parties, I have here. What the poet seeks in poetry and the painter in painting I have here. What the dictator seeks in power and the rich man in money and the drinker in wine, and what I too used to search for in vain, I have here. All my life is here, and all my world and all my loves. I have this great wealth and yet I possess nothing. I have all joy, all peace, all beauty and all love. I am satisfied and want nothing. I have you, and so I have all things, for you are lord of all, all stars, all countries, and all beings on earth.

My liver, my brain, my heart, all my organs and glands exist in order to love you. Everything on earth, poetry, beautiful women, beautiful country, wine, friendship, day and night were created to make me love you.

That I should love you with all my heart, with all my mind, with my imagination, with all the tenderness that is in me, with all the feeling and the poetry that is in me. That I should love you with all my passions and appetites and all my strength. And also with all my sweetness, all the passion and fire and longing for possession with which I used to love creatures. These creatures were tyrants over me. 'My mother's sons were angry with me, they made me keeper of the vineyards; but my own vineyard I have not kept' (Song of Solomon 1.6).

Unending moment

Suddenly the soul feels his presence unmistakably and cries
out with trembling fear: 'It's you who made heaven and
earth!' The soul tries to hide and vanish from his presence
but cannot. She cannot get away, God is all round her and
there is nowhere to escape to, for he is present throughout
heaven and earth and the soul too, totally. She is in his
arms. She who ran after happiness all her life and never
found it, seeking beauty and pleasure and joy, and wanting
to go on enjoying more and more and more, is now overwhelmed by an ocean of delight, boundless and fathomless.
It is too much. She cries: 'Enough, enough. If you love me
give me no more joy or I will die.' She is penetrated by such
an intense sweetness that it feels like pain, an indescribable
pain, infinitely bitter and infinitely sweet. Sometimes this
can all happen in a moment and never happen again for a
whole lifetime. But after this experience the soul finds that
all the beauty and pleasure and joys of the earth seem
empty. They are like 'dung', as the saints have said, (like
excrement, said St Paul). Now she can no longer enjoy
anything else but what she had at that moment, and sees that
from now on her life will be torture and martyrdom. She
has gone mad with love and is sick for the joy she tasted. She
will suffer torture till she tastes again, for another second,
this presence.

Friendship, wine, women, journeys, parties, all now seem empty forever, and the soul is now incapable of any other joy.

Within

Everyone has an inner room. Deep inside every human being there is a nuptial chamber where only the bridegroom comes. We all have within us a dark secret place, a locked room, created for love, an inner paradise. But most people do not know it is there.

So most people have an inner loveless emptiness. For human love, even the deepest, never reaches this secret place. It is the inner room. It is the place the bride speaks of in the Song of Songs, 'He took me into his chamber.' The bridegroom is knocking outside, as it says in Revelation: 'Behold I stand at the door and knock. If anyone hears my voice and opens the door, I will go in and sup with him and he with me.'

In the depths of his being everyone hears this call. It is the complaining voice that Nietzsche said he heard in his heart, which gave him pain and made him afraid. It is the voice in the Song of Songs: 'Open to me, my sister, my love, my dove, my perfect one; for my head is wet with dew, my locks with the drops of the night.' But the bride answers from her bed, 'I have put off my garment, how can I put it on? I have bathed my feet, how can I soil them?'

Most people have an empty room in their deepest being, like a painful voice that they sometimes hear crying in the silence of the night, or someone knocking at the door. Most people are sad inside. Outside they may smile and be merry. They turn outwards to answer the cry that comes from within them.

You have the kiss, the presence of love inside you and you are alone. If you turn inwards you will find it. But you do not know it because first you would have to go through the agony of giving up everything, even yourself. Your beloved is calling to you deep down inside you, or rather, in your deepest you, so deep that you think it is beyond you. He is deeper in you than your consciousness or your dreams.

And you are terrified of being alone. In the train or the doctor's waiting room or wherever you may be, you are terrified of being alone, without a book or a paper to read, with nothing to see or do or say. And all the while your best friend is knocking outside, his head wet with dew.

We were made for love, to love our maker. And time not spent in loving him is time wasted.

Love is the one law which rules the universe. It is the law that moves the sun and the other stars, as Dante says. It is the law by which all things hang together. Love is the stuff of which the universe is made. Every body in the universe attracts every other body by the force of its gravity. The earth attracts to itself every object on the earth and all these objects mutually attract one another. The earth attracts the moon and the sun attracts the earth and the moon and the other planets, and all the other stars in heaven, even the most distant. And all these other stars attract the sun and the planets and the earth and everything on the earth and all the other stars, each pulling strongly and each its own way. And every particle of matter in the universe attracts every other particle of matter. Even when two bodies are in an absolute vacuum, with no connexion between them, we know that they are strongly attracted to one another. Loving is being joined. Love is our only joy.

Every soul that God creates he creates loving. This was the restlessness in Augustine's heart, until he finally understood for whom his heart beat and whom he loved.

God is this feeling of great solitude and the knowledge that we have of a friend we are all born with.

And this friend is within us. He is where our dreams are, in the darkness of our subconscious, in the depths of our personality. He is in our secret self which we reveal to no one, not even to husband or wife, not even to ourselves. At the source of dreams, of myths, of love, there the beloved has his bridal chamber. When this chamber is empty, we are filled with loneliness, fear, melancholy and boredom. You may have a lot of money and property, securities in the bank, your house may have everything, but in yourself you can still be empty. If God is not there, the bitter wind of loneliness blows through you. Sometimes at night the soul, deprived so long of God's caress (sometimes after a night of pleasure or a party) wakes in terror at its own loneliness. At other times it wakes in the middle of the night and weeps.

Call

What we think of as reality, the reality we receive through our senses, is like a technicolour film. It is real but it is real like a technicolour film. Outside there is another reality. In the film there is love which can make us love and weep and forget that outside there is daylight and spring and real love and the voice of our beloved who calls in springtime: 'Arise my love and come, for the winter is over and gone.'

Yet we do not perceive this reality through our senses, but in the darkness of faith. This reality is like the electric current which runs darkly into our electric lamps, bringing them light. And this voice is like the waves of silent music which are carried through space across great distances.

We want God's voice to be clear but it is not. It is not clear because it cannot be clear to the senses. It is a deep, subtle and mysterious voice. It is like a deep yearning within us, at the root of the soul. It is a voice in the night. Vocation means called—by a voice in the night. A voice which calls us. We hear but we do not see. We want it to be clear as day but it is deep as night. It is deep and clear, but with a dark clarity like an X-ray. It reaches our bones.

For the voice of our beloved is existential, not verbal. It does not sound in our ears, or in our minds, but deeper, where he is present, in our deepest self. His call makes us discontented and sick of everything. He does not call us by words, but by events, circumstances, by reality. His call is not superficial and that is why it does not sound clear to us, because we live on the surface of ourselves, and there we communicate with one another in words. His call is deep, because God dwells in the depths of our being. His voice is silence.

God's call, vocation, is twofold. God calls us saying, 'Come and follow me.' We arrive and then we must follow. We find but must go on seeking. For as Gregory of Nyssa says, 'To find God is to seek him incessantly.' God's call is an incessant call, to the unknown, to adventure, to follow him in the night, in solitude. It is a call incessantly to go further, and further. For it is not static but dynamic (as his creation is also dyanamic) and reaching him means going on and on. God's call is like the call to become an explorer, it is an invitation to adventure.

It is the voice of the bird we hear in the night calling and calling. And another bird answers it much further away. One bird comes nearer and the other goes further off, still calling and calling. Then the voices of both birds are lost in the night.

Pleasure

Pleasure is a false god which says to us: surrender to me and I will satisfy you. But it never does satisfy us because we are greater than it. We cannot be satisfied with a pleasure that is less than infinite. We are leaking vases. Neither can we be satisfied with a beauty less than infinite. Every beauty which is not God is limited. 'In all perfection I saw a limit', cries the psalmist. This why beautiful things give us that deep feeling of melancholy, a painful sweetness.

Animals are satisfied with created things. They want nothing else. But people can only be satisfied with the infinite.

Every instinct in nature demands its rational satisfaction, and every natural need must be met. We are born with an instinct for the infinite, an instinct for God, and this instinct must be satisfied. This is the 'thirst for infinite illusions' spoken of by Darius.

Clinging to creatures brings frustration. A frustration as deep as that of the dictator deprived of power. Because it is clinging to something that does not belong to us, that we unjustly seek to dominate but which is snatched from our grasp.

But when we have tasted God we no longer desire the pleasure that comes from creatures. Just as at a banquet you would be repelled by the maggotty bread you welcomed in the concentration camp.

This light of truth, of what is real and authentic shining in all things, attracting us in all things, is God's light (He is infinitely shining truth because he is truth). The soft light of goodness glowing in all things and the brilliant light of beauty, which also attracts us in all things, are also God's light.

From him all stars get their light and all the beautiful hair in the world its shine. God is present in all things, burning in them without burning them up, like Moses' burning bush.

In the presence of anything beautiful, a beautiful woman, for example, you should think of the infinite beauty of your beloved who is the creator of all the beauty on earth and be freely glad that this beauty glorifies your God. You should not want to possess this beauty or take it away from your beloved, since he is for you and you are for him. Be glad at all this beauty because it is a hymn of praise to your beloved, and therefore a hymn of praise to you. For you are your beloved's and he is yours.

The earth is beautiful all over, Nicaragua, Venice, Kentucky, the Sahara. The sea is beautiful and also the desert, woods, plains, lakes, mountains, the tropics and the arctic. For everywhere God surrounds us with beauty and poetry, giving our eyes and all our sense the beauty he has created, the reflection and splendour of his invisible beauty.

All God's earth is beautiful; all the corners of it are delightful and all the beings on it are enchanting. But how are we to renounce this enchantment for his sake who is much more than all these things? And if the earth so charms us how are we to yearn to see God face to face?

I would go on foot to the ends of the earth if I thought I would meet you there. But you are within me and not at the ends of the earth.

You are within me and in your eyes are the eyes of all the girls I have loved and all the girls who have loved me and many others, and all the loving looks in the world and much more, and your eyes are fixed on me from all eternity, from all eternity they are looking at me.

Twofold

He who loves God wishes to be alone. Just as a newly married couple want to be alone and not have their intimacy interrupted by outsiders, those who have felt the love of God retire into silence and solitude.

'The soul cannot live without love,' says Catherine of Sienna. He who does not love God loves other things. The love we feel for God is the same as the love we felt before for other things. And he who loves God alone loves him with the love he used to feel for thousands of things, loves him with the strength of someone who loves only one thing in all the world, with a total and universal love.

Love is someone else dwelling within our person. Love is a presence. It is feeling we belong to someone else and that someone else belongs to us. Love is feeling that we are two but that the two are one. Love is knowing that we are loved, feeling the presence of the other loving us and smiling at us. Love is wanting to be someone else and knowing that we are someone else and that someone else wants to be us and that he is. Love is being emptied of ourselves and full of another. When we look at our beloved our whole soul is in our gaze. When we sigh, our whole soul is in our sigh. It is knowing that we make a pair and feeling at one with every pair we see, two lovers, two clouds, two doves flying past, two stars.

My feeling of solitude and my sighing in the night used to find no echo. It fell upon emptiness. I was alone. But now my sigh has found an echo, it reaches someone who hears it, someone I can neither see nor hear in the darkness. But I almost hear near me but within me, further within me than I am myself, his answering sigh.

And this someone is God. I understand your love and how you forgive me everything, because when I was in love before as much as you, I forgave everything, seventy times seven, and I know what your reactions are because I know what it is like to be in love. My former loves have taught me what love is. I know how you love me because I too have loved, and I know what passionate and obsessed love is and what it is to be madly in love with someone. And God is mad about me.

He loves me with all my weaknesses, with all my inherited and acquired defects, he loves me as I am, with my idiosyncrasies and my temperament, my habits and my complexes. Just as I am.

My soul is open. Someone else, not I, has the key. He comes and goes as he pleases.

Sex & marriage

'The kingdom of heaven is like a king who was making a wedding feast for his son...'

In heaven there will be no marriages, said Christ. That is, there will be no marriages between human couples because there will be no further need for children (the mystical body will be complete) and because there will be only one marriage: the wedding of the Lamb.

Heaven is marriage, hell is disappointed love. Human marriage is an image, a 'type' of heaven.

Sex is a symbol of divine love. It is a symbol and sacrament, and every profanation of it is sacrilege. As sacrament and symbol, it transcends its own material reality. It is more than it appears. It signifies a higher reality. It is a sign and what it signifies is divine love. That is why a Carthusian said monks renounce marriage for what marriage signifies.

The Song of Songs may have been originally a poem of human love (it must at least have been based on a human epithalamium). But divine inspiration made it symbolize divine love. Because all sexual love symbolizes divine love. For every poet who writes of his love, every love poem in the world and every human love (and even the irrational love of animals and the fertility of plants and the cohesive force of inanimate matter) are figure and type of divine love.

SEX & MARRIAGE 75

Marriage is so wonderful, so divine for us because it is the image of the divine marriage.

Loving God is to possess him. Loving God is to marry him.

People sometimes think there is a dilemma between whether to choose consecration to God or marriage. They do not know that consecration to God is marriage and that the soul who loves God 'marries' him, as St Bernard says.

The monk's eroticism is crucified and reborn. It goes on existing but it is transformed. The monk's is a pure passion; it is pure passion, with nothing in it but the passion and madness of love.

In every desire, in every appetite we have there is a huge quantity of energy, passion and fire. And how great is this energy and fire when the soul surrenders entirely to wanting one thing only, loving one thing only.

Passions, appetites, feelings, instincts and all the yearnings of the human heart are fuel for the love of God. Every human being can burn. And God's love for us is like throwing petrol on to a blazing fire.

Because when we feel we are loved by the person we love, we love more, and nothing inflames our love so much as to know we are loved by the person we love, and being loved more makes the other love more too. When we think about the person we love we love him more, and when we love him more we think about him more until we are nothing but one burning flame of love.

Every cell in our body, every particle of our being is nuptial, because we were made for marriage. All that Freud called the 'libido' is the oil in the lamps of the wise virgins awaiting the bridegroom.

St Maria Magadalen de Pazzi ran through the corridors of

her convent screaming wildly with love: 'Love! Love! Do you know sisters that Jesus is love and that he is mad with love?'

Anyone who has ever been madly in love can understand God's love. Divine love and human love are the same, only their object is different. The religious life is all about love.

The religious does not renounce creatures because they are bad, but rather because they are good and beautiful. They are so good and beautiful that they have made him fall in love with their creator. We know the creator's beauty through the beauty of his creatures ... and we have no other way of knowing his beauty.

If we have deprived ourselves of human beauty and human love, it is not because we despise them, but because they have inflamed us with the love of God. Did not God create sex and kissing and voluptuousness and passion? The creator of all things is not a barren God, as Isaiah says: 'Will I open the mother's womb for no children to be born? says the Lord. Will I close the womb, I who bring all things to birth? says your God.'

God is eternally young and new. His works are always fresh and the world starts again every morning as if it were newly created by him. Every dawn repeats his 'Let there be light' and has the freshness and newness of that first dawn. Through him the young colts leap with joy in the morning, the doves are glad and the mocking-birds sing: 'God the joy of my youth.' The charm and innocence of all young creatures come from him, source of virginity and fertility. He is the only love who does not grow old and the only lover who is not unfaithful and does not die.

Youth

Youth is the time to surrender to God, for it is the time for illusions, the time for love. The time for a man to love a woman, springtime and song of songs. Surrendering to God is surrendering in love. And at the time when you have most dreams and most illusions ('a thirst for infinite illusions') the gift you offer is greater and the gift you receive is greater, and the mutual love is greater. If you were disappointed with your life, what life would you have to give? God wants youth and fervour and passion and dreams. He asks from you what marriage would demand, because his love is marriage.

The marriage is of the whole church with Christ, and of each particular soul with Christ, for in each soul the whole church is present, as the body of Christ is complete in each eucharistic host and in the bodies of all Christians. So in a hermit's cave the whole church is present, militant, suffering and triumphant. And in the solitude of each soul that marries Christ, Christ is complete, and as all men are in Christ, in each soul that marries Christ, Christ is present together with all men, that is the whole mystical body of Christ, 'the whole Christ', as Augustine says.

'... It is like a king who made a wedding feast for his son.' But those who were invited first did not come. We are these who were invited later, the blind and the lame from the highways and byways who were asked instead. And who were these first guests who did not come. Surely they were the great men of this world, governors, prime ministers, bank directors, film stars, big businessmen, famous writers, men of a will of iron and those with the gift of leadership, men with money or great things, men adored by women. These are the ones who refused the invitation to the wedding, because they had important things to do, previous engagements or appointments, and a lot of letters to write, or they did not read the invitation among all the letters they received, or because they themselves were getting married that day.

Journey

When we want to go towards our creator we turn towards creatures, like the butterfly that bumps into the window pane. For creation is transparent and the splendour of God shines through it.

We turn outwards attracted by the beauty we see in created things, without realizing that they are only a reflection of the real beauty. And the real beauty is within us. And so, paradoxically, the more we turn towards beauty, the more we turn away from it. For it is in the opposite direction. We turn outwards and it is within.

But we cannot be joined to God and then leave all created things. First we must leave all things and then we can be joined to God.

God cannot join our soul until we have consented, just as the lover cannot be joined to his love, however much he loves her, while she still loves others. But God is joined to our soul the very moment the soul loves him. It is an automatic union. As soon as the soul stops loving creatures, it is suspended, not in the void, because there is no void, but in the bottomless abyss which is God. The soul is automatically embraced by God.

And just as we cannot pour wine into a jug which is already full, unless we empty it, the soul cannot be filled by God if it is not first emptied of everything else.

But before receiving God's embrace we must endure the

pain of being detached from everything else. We must become detached from all our desires and appetites, from everything we cling to and only then will our arms be free to receive God.

Love always presses the lover towards union with his love, and so God who loves our soul from all eternity immediately joins it, without waiting a moment longer, as soon as there is no obstacle separating it from him.

The process of detachment may take place slowly over a number of years or can happen all in a moment. But God bursts in violently the moment the soul is alone, horribly alone, detached from the whole created universe, suspended in a sort of void between creation and God. Then the soul is flooded by God, for as St John of the Cross says, there is no vacuum in the universe and emptying ourselves of all things means filling ourselves with God. But even if the soul has one single attachment left, one single affection for what is not God, then God cannot come in. For if there is one single affection, the soul will be set on this, for it must embrace something, and then it will not be free for God. First we must go through the agony of possessing nothing created, then we fall into God. First we must die.

While we do not surrender completely to God, neither does he surrender completely to us. The sacrifice is supreme. But the reward is also supreme. We exchange the multitude of particular, finite and fleeting beauties, for absolute infinite and eternal beauty.

The journey to God is like an interplanetary flight which becomes more and more difficult as we go further from earth's gravity, but once we are out of range of earth's gravity becomes easier and easier, as we are drawn more and more by the gravity of the planet which is our destination.

Source

Nature is religious in its very essence. The starry sky is a prayer, so is every beautiful bit of country and the silence of lonely places.

Crickets speak to us of God as well as the stars. Both the crickets and the stars tell us about him who created them.

The whole universe yearns for union with God, and has done ever since it came forth from God. All things are scattered away from God and long to join each other. The law of love is the one physical and biological law of the universe and the one moral law ('A new commandment I give to you: that you should love one another as I have loved you').

All our desires and hungers, for food, sex, friendship, are a single appetite, a single hunger, for union with one another and with the universe. It is a cosmic communion which finds fulfilment only in Christ ('when I am raised on high, I will draw all things to me'). And when Christ returned to the Father, we all returned with him. Christ told us about this cosmic return in the parable of the prodigal son.

We came from God's bosom. We were as much part of him as the foetus is part of its mother. And we return to him just as a man returns to woman, from whom he came.

In the meanwhile our soul cries to God as the calf cries for its mother, and the mother cow calls her calf.

We go towards God as the moth at night makes for the flame. And as fishes rise to the surface of the water attracted by the torch of the fisherman who is waiting above with his harpoon. Or like the stag dazzled by the lamp the hunter is shining at him.

We are born loving and when we open our eyes we see the reflection everywhere of him we love, but we do not see him we love. So things drive us mad with love.

All things both charm and disappoint us. They charm us because they are a reflection and image of God. They disappoint us because they are an image but not the reality: they are not God.

There is nothing ugly in the universe. There is only beauty and the relative absence of beauty, the relative absence of the divine reflection in a particular thing.

Beauty, joy and pleasure are spread through things. All things are illuminated by beauty to a greater or lesser degree, like a light diffused over all things. But God is not spread or diffused, he is the light source.

Things have beauty to a greater or lesser degree but they are not beauty. God is the light bathing beautiful bodies, and in him there is nothing which is not this beauty. This is why when we have tasted God, every other beauty or pleasure becomes insipid and unsatisfying. Every delight leads us to seek for God, the source of all delight and all beauty.

All the beauty we see is like a trickle of water which leads us back to its source. The beauty of red hair leads us back to its source. What is the marvellous origin of this beauty, where does this being I love come from? What is he like from whom all this beauty comes?

Girls' smiles, flowers, the fishes of the sea, the moving stars are fleeting beauties which come from God, shine in our sight for a moment and return to the depths of him who created them. Why do we go on seeking these fleeting beauties and not turn to the inexhaustible source of all beauty, the hearth from which all these sparks of beauty come, sparkle and fall?

Things have their supreme existence in God. Everything that exists has its existence in God. And the realities we see are like shadows of all that is God. The reality we see is as unreal compared to the reality in God as a coloured photograph compared to what it represents.

Butterflies, snow, mountains are reflections of a divine perfection which exists to the highest degree in God, pre-eminently. In God there is an infinite butterfly, infinite snow, infinite mountains, which are the archetypes of those we see here, and which are God's very essence, which are God. The things we see here are limited, finite, contingent and individual but in God the butterfly, the snow and the mountains are one same concentrated infinite thing. The butterfly archetype and the mountain archetype in God are the same archetype because they are the same God who is infinite and thus everything at once. They are the same simple thing which is God.

God shines in matter, although he is infinitely far from matter, and although matter is opaque and composed of gross atoms. The reflection of God's supreme beauty is what produces other beauties scattered here and there, the blue sea, the seagull, the beauty of women and of herons, and quiet green tropical rivers flowing under green palms in the evening light.

What will it be like to see this beauty in itself, unveiled, face to face and not reflected in resistant matter but as it is concentrated in God? There you will see the beauty you saw in the sea and in women and snow and the heron, but not scattered in transitory individual reflections, concentrated in one thing, in one being.

These are the scattered pages of the book of the universe which Dante says in his last canto he saw put together again into one book by love.

This is the beam of light in which St Benedict in his ecstasy saw the universe contained.

The plane flying through the sky, the car running along the road, the wood, flowers, girls, the Divine Comedy, everything that exists, has an eternal existence in God. But in God they are not separate and individual things as they are in their present reality as creatures, but they are one single essence, God's very essence, they are God. Here things exist separately, a flower, love, a poem, a piece of music. In God flower, love, poem and music are one infinite, one pure act.

The contemplation of God is a recapitulation and synthesis of all creatures. But all must die to return to their origin, to the unity of all things which is God. And we must renounce everything, including ourselves who are part of this everything, to return to the All. Only by dying to ourselves can we find our identity because our identity is not in ourselves but in the All. Our centre is in God who is also the centre of all things. And communicating with all things is also finding ourselves, and finding ourselves is being united with all things. Surrendering ourselves is finding ourselves and to lose ourselves is to be saved ('He who saves his life will lose it and he who loses his life for love of me will save it'). We live in a paradoxical universe.

Our self is solitude and he who resists suffering and dying, who does not want to give himself but to hang on to himself, remains outside the unity of all things which is God. ('If the grain of wheat does not die, it remains alone . . .')

Structures

As the soul of the artist is reflected in his work of art, so created things reflect God in their inmost structure. Go into the fields in the early morning and notice things, the smells, the colours, the birdsong. In all this there is a reflection of God.

Everything in nature has a trade mark, God's trade mark. The stripes on a shell and the stripes on a zebra; the grain of the wood and the veins of the dry leaf; the markings on the dragonfly's wings and the pattern of stars on a photographic plate; the panther's coat and the epidermis cells of the lily petal; the structure of atoms and galaxies. All bear God's finger prints.

There is a *style*, a divine style in everything that exists, which shows that everything was created by the same artist. Everything is multiplicity within unity. Everything is both like other things and individual. Every individual thing has its own manner of being; it is that and not anything else, but at the same time there are millions and millions of others like it, both minute creatures and stars. Everything has its own stripes, speckles, spots, dapples, veins or grain, the caterpillar, the clay pot, the chameleon, the Klee painting and the Persian carpet, sea spray, stalactites, white agate veins in pebbles, the carpet of autumn leaves, wood, marble, the shell of the foraminifera and the skeleton of the radiolarian.

They all have God's finger-prints. This is the seal of the Trinity of God three in one, infinite multiplicity in infinite unity, the unity of what is distinct.

In the image of God who created them, all beings are one and many at the same time, all beings from the galaxy to the electron.

No two caterpillars are alike, no two atoms, no two stars, even though they look the same in the sky at night. But everything also has something in common. Poetry must discover this pattern, this design running throughout creation, and see how even the most different things have likenesses. The mountains skip like rams and the hills like young sheep. Your hair is a flock of goats winding through the mountains of Gilead.

Sin & unfreedom

The chorus of frogs and crickets on moonlit nights, the cries and calls and complaints of all animals, the cock crowing in the distance, the mooing cow, the barking dog and all other mysterious country sounds, are a divine office just like the monk's. They are psalms in another language. They are also prayer.

Birds sing asking the Father for their food every day, and that his will be done on earth as it is in heaven, and they bless his name and all other animals also pray the Our Father in their own way.

Every work of art also praises God. And gives glory to God like the stars which proclaim the glory of God in the heavens. All true art is also a sort of prayer. Art does not have to be religious to give glory to God, because all art is religious.

God's holiness is manifest everywhere, even in pigs' eyes.

Everything in nature is pure, tubercular spit and the clear waters surrounding the islands in the Caribbean (and so St Catherine of Genoa drank pus and St Luis Rey kissed the wounds of lepers). Worms and herons are both pure and lovely. All matter is pure and holy because it comes from God's hands. Everything is pure except sin. Everything is pure except our fallen nature. A landscape is pure because it has no appetites to be disordered like fallen man. And animals are pure because they are not proud or overbearing. And when a person is a saint, when he has no disordered appetites, and is neither proud nor overbearing, his rational soul becomes as pure as woods and lakes, worms and herons.

An animal or a tree is the exact image of an idea in the mind of God (God's mind is his essence because everything in God is God's essence). Each is a faithful message expressing precisely what God wanted to express by it and nothing more. Every material thing is perfect obedience. Every thing faithfully fulfils in its being that God wants it to be. Every star, as the prophet Baruch says, is saying in heaven 'Here I am!' All irrational things are the fulfilment of God's desire.

The human body is also holy and cannot sin. Only our will can sin and where there is no will there is no sin.

The presence of God in all things means that when we sin God is a spectator and he who is infinite innocence is forced to become our accomplice in sin as well as our victim. This is why sin is sin.

Sinning is tyrannizing over God. But it is also tyrannizing over ourselves as well as God. The damned have tyrannized over themselves eternally and committed enormous injustice against themselves. Sin is not free, it is the surrender of freedom, but sin makes us feel we are exercising our freedom just as the propaganda of dictators claims they are the 'people's government'. Many think they are free because they do as they 'like', but they do not realize that they are being dictated to from within and this dictator governs their will and makes them do what they do not want to do, even though they think they want it. So they repent of what they have done, because they have done what they did not want and they do not want what they have done. They think they are free because the dictatorship is from within, it is installed at the very centre of their will. The tyrant is within and they think they themselves are the tyrant when they are his slaves. And when a man like this rules a people, that people is ruled by a dictatorship. The greed, pride, cruelty and hatred which dominate the tyrant also dominate the country. They are the prime minister or the president of the people.

Poverty

Adam was naked in Eden. So poverty is the paradisal state. Adam was as poor as the animals, like Francis and like Christ.

After the fall man could no longer be naked, but a monk's habit is the clothing most like the paradisal nakedness.

Poverty is also truth, riches are disguise. We put on clothes to cover ourselves and to hide our inner nakedness. Falsehood and riches are synonymous.

Riches are also a falsification of things. A rich dress, a rich house falsify the original authenticity of the materials, they hide the natural nakedness of things, they cheat.

But there is a splendour in poor things, the splendour of what is real. A rich thing is always less real than a poor thing. That is why Thoreau said that it was important for a man to be able to go out wearing patched trousers. The splendour of poor things made of clay, straw, homespun or plain wood, the coarse, the rough, the crude, the common is the nakedness of matter. It is like the splendour of the naked body. Such things have the same simple splendour as works of art, texture and colour.

If man had not lost his innocence he could go naked. Francis' only possessions were a pair of sandals, a sack and a girdle (and sometimes he even left those off).

The deceitfulness of riches is the confusion between what we have and what we are. We think we are more because we have more. We buy a car and think the car has become part of ourselves, like an extra limb. Thus Augustine said that giving up riches hurt like losing a limb. And if someone admires our car, we feel that they are admiring us. We think of the things we have as part of ourselves, like a mollusc with a shell that does not belong to it. So the possession of things is a falsification of ourselves.

The rich man thinks he is what he has. He shows off his things to be admired for them as if they were him. He wants to be valued for what he has rather than what he is. The Latin poet Propertius saw the true value of poverty when he boasted he had won a girl by his poems and not by his possessions.

Riches are a deception. Anyone who thinks he owns a parcel of the earth of this planet through a title deed is as mad as the people in the United States who are now staking claims to land on the moon through deeds granted them by some fraudulent agency. A wood or a meadow is owned by the birds and animals that enjoy it, by the loving couple who walk there or the hermit who lives there, not by the man who has the title deed. He only possesses a scrap of official paper disfigured by ugly legal prose.

We possess the whole of nature and all the earth and all countries and the starry sky. But we lose all this if we limit our sense of property to a number of acres of land. We can only possess the universe by being poor, as the birds who are poor possess the sky and the fishes who are poor possess the water, and as Francis possessed all things. That is why Francis called poverty a great treasure ('we are not worthy of so great a treasure!'). He said the greatest luxury was to sit and eat on a beautiful rock by a stream under the blue sky. The poor rich people only had a dining room where they were shut in.

We are sons of God and he is lord of all. As his sons we are also lords of all the riches in the world. We are surrounded by fabulous riches and we have only to stretch out our hand and take them. A handful of clear water flowing through my fingers is not worth less than a handful of diamonds. We only appreciate it less because it is more abundant. A golden fish in the lake, a jade green frog, a shining pebble, a stick floating in the water, all these are treasures, although no one will put a fictitious money value on them.

Anyone who buys a field and puts a fence round it, loses all the rest of nature and everything else. So religious poverty does not mean possessing little but not possessing anything, total dispossession in order to possess everything. We do not limit ourselves to the legal possession of a few things by virtue of a scrap of paper. For what is more ours than the air, the sun, the earth, the sky and the sea?

And poverty is also a virtue of the Trinity because God's life is communal and communist and each of the three divine persons gives himself totally to the others, and in the Trinity there is no mine or yours, even though there is I and you.

The deceitfulness of riches also lies in thinking that material things can be embraced by a spiritual being like the soul. In Nicaragua we had a dictator who could not satisfy his lust for land. He grabbed more and more land but was never satisfied because although he held the title deeds the land still did not become his, and however much he grabbed, he remained as poor as he was before, and so he went on wanting more and more. The green fields with their cows and trees and the stream which meandered across them remained as unpossessed as they had been before. He had the title deeds to the land but it was not his. Whoever walked over it and enjoyed the view, or fished in the river, and then went away without coveting more, possessed the land, although he may have been a poor man with no title deeds.

Only by not coveting, only by giving up everything can we possess everything. That is why Paul says that whoever has anything should behave as if he did not, and whoever buys anything should behave as if he had not, and whoever marries should behave as if he had not.

Materialism & idolatry

Money is a tyranny, or as Christ said in the language of antiquity, it is a 'master' (which for the ancients also meant a god). 'No man can serve two masters...' Then he goes on to call money by the name of the god of Sidon, Mammon, for money is also an idolatary: '...God or Mammon.'

On another occasion Christ identifies money with another form of totalitarianism and another god; 'Render to Caesar the things that are Caesar's and to God the things that are God's.' In saying this he was not legitimizing the things that are Caesar's, as many have thought, nor was he putting two equally legitimate orders side by side: God's and Caesar's. The irony of the phrase is obvious, the money is not Caesar's, it merely has his image on it, but Christ says that it is Caesar's because of this. Christ is saying that money is not ours but Caesar's and we are God's. 'Render to Caesar the things that are Caesar's' means: Leave the money to Caesar ... it is rubbish. 'Render to God the things that are God's' means that we should surrender ourselves to God because we are his and bear his image.

Money belongs to tyranny, cruelty, pride and idolatry, to Tiberius. All coins and notes have Tiberius' picture on them. (That is why Francis forbade his friars to handle money.)

The first of the ten commandments, not to make graven images or worship idols, sounds to us like a commandment for primitive peoples still at the stage of polytheism, an archaeological relic with no relevance to civilized man.

But modern materialism is the same as ancient polytheism, and the world has never had as many idols as it has now. Cars, film stars, political leaders, ideologies, these are modern idols. City streets and motorways are full of idols, the idols of commercial and political propaganda, the smiling deities of wealth and abundance, of nutrition and hygiene, the gods of beer and cornflakes and toothpaste, or the faces of dictators and political leaders, the dark divinities of terror and war, destruction and death.

And the same forces of nature worshipped by primitive man without understanding in fire and thunder are also worshipped by modern man in electricity and atomic energy, without understanding.

Possession

From microcosm to macrocosm, all creation speaks of God's infinity. We should see all things as symbols and images, as photographs of God. Not as things valuable in themselves, to be possessed and enjoyed for themselves.

Possessing God means becoming detached from things. Becoming detached from things is embracing God.

And only God can be possessed. If I see a thing I like and I buy it, I do not then possess it. Even though I can give it away or sell it, I have not therefore possessed it. The thing remains inviolate because our faculty of possession lies deep within us, where external things cannot reach. That is why all those who possess things are dissatisfied. This dissatisfaction cannot be cured (only made worse) by possessing yet more things.

There is a sort of invisible glass wall between us and things. We dash against it like butterflies but we cannot pass through. Outside the window the world goes on smiling at us untouched, unreached.

And we cannot possess the people we love. They (and we) remain inviolate in their deepest selves. Even between husband and wife there is always a certain distance. They do not become completely one, even though they may wish it. They have only the illusion of union.

Only God can be possessed. He alone can come into our

deepest self, and that is where we possess and are possessed. He alone has the key.

He does not come from outside but from inside. He enters our castle by secret passages communicating with him.

And we can join him without going out of ourselves. Indeed we can only join him by being within ourselves.

Does that mean we can never possess creatures? This might disturb us for all eternity, because we would still remember creatures, and not lose the memory of them for all eternity and we would be tormented by the memory of what we might never possess. Yes we can possess creatures, but in God. By possessing God we possess everything, because he possesses all things. All things came from God and will return to God in Christ. 'When I am lifted on high I will draw all things to me,' said Christ. And when all things are drawn to him they will also be drawn to me, for he is more me than I am myself, he is my deepest self.

But first we must renounce all things. That is why St John of the Cross said the way to possess all things is to be dispossessed of all things.

Meanwhile we are like birds shut in a room beating against the glass wall. They see before them a country in lovely light but they cannot get out. Thus we beat against creatures, we are deceived because we see God through them. But we crash into them because they are solid and do not allow us to pass through to God. Only God's light passes through them. And only by turning aside from this light shining through creatures, only by turning back towards the dark can we find the way out to the garden, to freedom and light, to God.

Appearances

Protons and neutrons dance forming marvellous shapes before our eyes, like the shapes in a kaleidoscope. But the shapes are illusory, they are only coloured chips shining for a moment in the light which is God.

This whole world is made of shadows, shadows on the wall of a cave, as Plato said. Shadows on a cinema or television screen we would say.

Like film stars we see singing and laughing on a screen, who are not real but only an image made of light and shade, the stars in the sky smiling and singing in the night are also shadows. Sometimes they may even be stars which no longer exist. They have been dead for millions of years, even though their light still reaches us, just like film stars who died long ago, but whom we still see laughing and singing on the screen.

We perceive fleeting images, with our eyes, our ears, through our sense of touch, on the screen of our senses, but this is not reality. Death will be the end of the programme for us and return to reality. Meanwhile we gape at the world like children gaping at the television.

Reality is God, who is dark, who cannot be perceived through the senses or through the mind or the imagination. We can only apprehend him as something dark beyond the senses, the imagination and the mind, in the darkness of faith. Although faith is not darkness but an invisible light penetrating reality beyond the light we see, like an X-ray.

Soul

God's presence is a dark and invisible presence, like the presence of another person we sometimes feel in a dark room.

We have often felt his presence within us without realizing it, believing that it is ourselves. Sometimes it is a feeling of loneliness or fear, a sense of silence, a mysterious love rushing up inside us.

After a party or a dance, when you come home to your room in the small hours and are alone, perhaps in the silence you sometimes feel the presence of someone, a sad face near you which is not you. And you feel your emptiness. You are afraid to look in the mirror, knowing that what you see is not you, that your face is a mask. You are afraid to look at yourself face to face because it is like looking at a corpse. You are afraid to be alone, by yourself. It is like the fear you feel in an empty house.

You feel that you, you alone in the universe, are far away from God. The galaxies slowly revolving through their courses for millions of years, and the slow geological evolution of the earth and all the flora and fauna of the sea and the flora and fauna of the earth, obey his law, and you do not obey.

But this will of God that you do not obey is not outside you. It is not imposed on your will from the outside. It is more your own than your own will, and more you than you are yourself, your deepest self and truest identity and the ultimate will of your being.

We feel the beloved's presence in the darkness, his mysterious caress. He is present within us but we do not see him. We only see material reality, a reality as false as technicolour films and the advertisements on television.

Sometimes even when I was far from God a faint face came into my dreams, or when I was alone in the silence of the night, after parties. It was the God I had neglected and relegated to the darkness of my unconscious. But he was imprinted on my soul, faint and sorrowful like the face of Christ printed on Veronica's veil. My pain, my dream, my terror in the night was this face on Veronica's veil.

Love is inside us, drawing us to the centre of ourselves, which he is. For love always seeks union, the identification of the lover and the beloved. There is someone within me who is not me. We are made in such a way that God is the centre of our being. In such a way that to turn in on ourselves is to draw near to God. Even though we cannot reach him because the distance between us and him is infinite, he is also infinitely close to us, infinitely within.

Image

We are living portraits of God, works of art. Our deepest mystery, the ultimate secret of our being is that we are not just ourselves, we are images. Our essence is not to be ourselves, but a copy, a photograph of another. Only when we reflect this other are we ourselves. We are a white screen upon which God is projected. If the film is taken away, nothing remains.

This duality is the secret of our being. There is something within us which is the All, and at the same time we are nothing. We are a nothing upon which the All projects itself. But we can blur the image of this All. The soul in a state of sin is the Nothing.

On the one hand we are children of Nothing, and on the other children of God, because God made us out of nothing. Nothing and God, that is the duality within us.

We came from God, in whom we were from all eternity, we were part of God, and we shall never be satisfied until we return to God. Meanwhile we are in exile. We are persons displaced from God. But is is also true that we came from nothing. For when we were in God we were not ourselves but God; becoming ourselves meant coming out of nothing. We were born of chaos made fertile by God. This infinite nothing, this chaos from which we come, is what the saints see inside themselves when they also see God, and is the reason for their terror and humility. They see within themselves this nothing, which is total absence, lack of everything, the very essence of rotting and decay, of autumn, death and forgetfulness. We are made of this, of aging, autumn, the stuff of death, of corpses; we wither and perish.

Hunger and plague and the horrors of war give us an idea of what we also are. For if we destroy the image of God projected onto us, we become the face of melancholy, pain and death. Beneath every being lies a corpse, grinning. In the darkness of our depths we may laugh, but our laugh is the grin on the faces of the dead in the mortuary freezers. This is what children are afraid of in the dark, and the child that remains within us goes on being afraid in the darkness of the dream world, the nothingness from which we came and which we are, the dust we came from and to which we shall return, because we are still dust. The life within us is superficial and intermittent. We are dead when we sleep and even when we are awake we are asleep or dead to many things. The artist's struggle is merely the struggle to maintain this life artificially. And the lover tries to safeguard this life from routine and death by means of his love. For everything passes and everything must submit at last to the stillness of death. Art also passes and becomes empty. Beauty grows old and fades, and love grows cold. Everything in the universe is subject to the second law of thermodynamics. God alone is the living God, eternal life, the ever new, the perpetual freshness of the morning. For he is he who is. He does not have life, he is life. 'If anyone thirst, let him come to me and drink. He who believes in me, as the scripture has said, "Out of his heart shall flow rivers of living water."' (Jn. 7.37–8.)

Will of God

Everything that happens is a sacrament of God's will. As the body of Christ is hidden beneath the appearances of bread and wine, God's will is hidden beneath the appearances, the bread and wine, of day to day happenings.

Every historical event is as sacred as the sacred Scriptures, because it is also an expression of the will of God. And the humblest everyday event is also an expression of God's will and therefore as important as the grandest historical event. Missing a train is as important as Napoleon losing the battle of Waterloo.

So there is nothing banal or insignificant in the world ('Every hair on your head is counted'). The most banal event can change the whole history of the world. A falling tile caused the death of a king of Spain. And the child selling newspapers today may make eight columns tomorrow in every newspaper in the world. But every other banal event also helped shape the history of the world, even if we did not notice it, and the life of every man is equally important, even if it does not get into the papers.

Our quiet daily life is full of meaning and mystery, and is like a hidden continuation of the hidden years spent by Jesus in Nazareth. Although these years are not described in the gospels they are not therefore less important – just like the other doings of Jesus which are not recorded in the

Gospels, and which, as John says, 'were every one of them to be written the world itself could not contain the books that would be written'.

What we call sacred history is only a fragment—inspired by the Holy Spirit—of universal sacred history—the intervention of God's will in the world. All history is sacred, and so are the things that happen in our private lives. The Sacred Scriptures from Genesis to Revelation are an illuminated strand running right through human history, from the beginning to the end of the world, from the first day to the last. The rest of the history of the world (and other inhabited worlds if they exist) is not illuminated, it is a plain text. But the will of God is not therefore less present in this text.

But this text can be altered by man, and man has altered it a great deal, ever since the first sin. Sacred history is also the history of the will of God constantly modified by man. God decided to bring Israel to the promised land. When the people murmured and wanted to go back to Egypt God changed his plans. He decided to exterminate these people and create a new people for Moses. Moses besought God to spare the people of Israel and God once again apparently changed his mind. He would not exterminate them but neither would they enter the promised land as he had first intended. 'Not one shall come into the land where I swore that I would make you dwell.' (Num. 14.30.)

God's will is an intricate pattern which is constantly being modified by the free will of man, but is still not destroyed. At each moment God's will is changing to fit circumstances changed by us.

In every particular case God's will takes into account the innumerable consequences which will follow from it and alter all the other cases and circumstances in the universe. When I pray for rain for my harvest or for it to stop raining so that I can keep an appointment, I am only thinking of rain or fine from my own point of view. But God thinks of all the effects and consequences of rain or fine throughout the world. God's will is the sum of all these things thought of at the same time by infinite wisdom and infinite love. So we should gladly accept everything that happens because everything that happens, however unpleasant it appears, is for our good.

The only thing that is not good for us is sin, because sin alone depends on us and not on the will of God. Sin is against the will of God and is the enemy.

But everything that does not depend on our will is the will of God. Even the effects and consequences of sin are the will of God, although the sin itself was our will, and the effects and consequences of the sins of others are also the will of God. A man fires a gun at another man by his own will, but whether the revolver is loaded, whether the bullet comes out, the path of the bullet, whether it hits its mark, and all the other consequences of this man's action depend on the will of God. So we should bless everything that happens, for all things, even the effects of sin, are the will of God, and the only thing that is not is our consenting to sin.

Sometimes we do not want to recognize the will of God because it comes to us in hideous disguise, as some Jews did not wish to recognize their king when Pilate presented him to them crowned with thorns. They preferred the dictatorship of Tiberius: 'We have no king but Caesar!' (the Caesar that later smashed them, whereas Christ was their liberator). The will of God sometimes comes to us in the form of disaster, misery, loneliness and death. And we prefer Tiberius who is power, pleasure, money, cruelty and glory. And we cry: 'Crucify him! We have no king but Caesar!'

The will of God can appear in the form of cancer, or a road accident, or the police of a totalitarian state arresting you in the night, and it is difficult to recognize and bless God in these disguises. But all that we call *reality* is the incarnation of the word of God, what God wishes. All reality is sacred. A chance meeting in the street, missing a train or aeroplane, they are all the will of God.

God is present not only in the bread and wine of the eucharist but also in some way in all corn, and all wine and all water and all oil and all reality. God is silently and humbly present in reality, because all reality is a sacrament.

We do not know what is good for us and we should neither want nor not want anything except what God wants or does not want for us. We should accept things as God sends them, because he knows what is good for us. Things happen all round us which we do not understand, we do not know where they come from or where they are going, like a blind person in busy traffic. We are like a small child at a large airport full of planes arriving and leaving, and the child cannot get on the plane he wants because he does not know where any of them are going and he does not know where he is going himself. He has to wait to be told which plane he is meant to get on. We do not know our destination, nor what is good for us, which things that happen do us good or evil, because we do not know the future (and we only know the past and the present in a very partial way).

But sin is believing that we know better than God what

is good for us, that God is mistaken on some particular point about us, that what God wants for us in this particular case is wrong for us.

Only God knows what is good for us, because everything that happens and will happen has already happened in his mind for all eternity, like a photograph taken long ago which we now see for the first time in the dark room, or like a film already made but which we now see on the screen, or like the light given out by a star millions of years ago but which only now reaches our retina.

God knows that what does not suit me today may suit me tomorrow. And God may want something now that he does not want later, or want something here that he does not want somewhere else, or want something for me that he does not want for others. When they asked Joan of Arc at her trial whether God loved the English, she replied: 'God does not love the English *in* France'. And this is the mystery of our vocation. God also loves the man who is dictator of Nicaragua, but he does not love him *as* the dictator of Nicaragua.

Miracles

We live surrounded by miracles we do not realize. Not only miracles in the conventional sense, but also natural miracles. No one loves nature more than God the creator of nature, and he wishes his miracles to be ordinary. He the cause of causes prefers all things to have a cause and causes to have their effects and it all to happen naturally.

Everything that happens has a meaning, and the ordinary is as meaningful as the miracle. A rat is a miracle, as Whitman says. Everything ordinary is a miracle, all the more marvellous because we do not pay attention to it. It is the humble unseen miracle of every day.

That is why Augustine said that the miracle of the multiplication of the bread was no greater than the miracle that happens every day in every seed. It was only less 'usual'.

Creation was not an isolated act by God, remote in time, but it is a perennial act which is happening before our eyes at every moment, and also before the eyes of unbelievers and even then they do not believe. We are being created at every moment, brought out of nothing all the time. The whole universe is a perpetual miracle, and the most ordinary everyday events are as miraculous as the miracles at Lourdes.

The ordinary is God's ordinary way of working miracles. It is as miraculous as the extraordinary, but we do not see it so because we are used to it. But for those who live in contact with God, all their life is extraordinary and supernatural and full of miracles.

God works visible miracles to show the world, but within the soul he does not need to work miracles of that kind. He works them through coincidence and everyday events, which are also miraculous but not in the showy way.

Sometimes it is difficult for us to tell the difference between a miracle and a coincidence. This is because a coincidence can also be a miracle; God can work miracles by means of coincidence.

In fact nothing happens by chance. What we call chance is really another name for the will of God. Sometimes it is difficult for us to recognize the will of God because it is incarnate in reality, in the natural laws of history, physical phenomena, accidents, chance, luck, coincidence. All this is God's providence.

We usually only call the extraordinary happenings in our life providential, and only those things that suit us or that we think suit us. We think it providential if we escape unharmed from a road accident, or if we did not take the plane which crashed. We do not realize that being killed in a road accident or being on the plane which crashes are also providential. Fundamentally this is a residual manichaeism, believing that there are two gods, good and evil, and that providence is the victory of the good God over the god of catastrophe and chaos. But there is only one God and nothing in the universe escapes his providence except sin. And everything that happens is providential, and everything that happens is good for us except sin. Only sin is not providential, because it is the one thing that is not made by God but by man, even though the effects and consequences of sin which do not depend on men but on God are provi-dential. Providential means the unfavourable as well as the favourable, the ordinary as well as the extraordinary, what does not happen as well as what happens.

We often do not recognize providence because our will intervenes and goes against the will of God, and we go against providence. But if we attach our will to the will of God and do not the slightest thing against his plans, then we see divine providence acting in our lives in the most marvellous way, and chance and the unexpected and all our daily life are full of meaning; all our life is full of the most amazing coincidences and miracles.

If you never do your will in anything but only the will of God, then every meeting in the street, every telephone call, every letter you get will be full of meaning and you will find it makes sense and that it follows a providential plan.

Most people feel themselves alone in the universe and un-protected, as if their only providence were themselves, as if they had been created by themselves or by chance and they lived in a universe ruled by chance. They feel poor and helpless in a hostile world, like children lost in a wood, and not like beings created by God and placed by God in a benevolent universe also created by him for us. We are not alone; he who created us dwells within us and surrounds us outside. When we say 'Our Father' with faith and love we are at home even in the vast spaces between the stars and the galaxies.

When we realize that he who governs the course of the stars, and the galaxies and the expansion of the universe is also he who controls the circulation of our blood and our metabolism and our lowliest daily doings, then we shall feel secure and confident and calm. He takes care of the glow worm as well as the galaxies, and not an atom moves without his consent. So what in the universe shall we fear?

The physical laws of the universe and the moral law are all one law. Only the moral law is a law of God that can be broken by men. We cannot break the laws of God's creation in thermodynamics, for example, but we can break the moral law. Man is the only part of the universe who can disobey. And when we obey the will of God we are in harmony with all the rest of the universe, because we are obeying the same law that all physical nature obeys. Because all non-human creatures obey their creator, as Baruch says: 'He that sends forth light, and it goes, calls it again and it obeys him with fear. The stars shine in their watches and rejoice. When he calls them, they say, "Here we are"; and so with cheerfulness they show light unto him that made them.' (Baruch 3.33–5.)

Joy can also be a perfect prayer, because it is an act of confidence in God, and the certainty that nothing evil can happen to us in the universe. And joy can sometimes also be heroic.

Damnation &
self-denial

Sin is wanting to be gods, little limited finite gods, but still gods. Or like gods. That is, wanting to be the centre of the universe and be our own lawgiver.

Sin is becoming a law to ourselves and abandoning the law of God. Sin is tyranny, becoming a dictator over ourselves, because disobeying God, as St Bernard says, is becoming a tyrant over ourselves. The damned man has been unjust to himself, because he has condemned his own innocent being to be deprived of God eternally, to be nothing, and that is why God hates a damned man, who hates himself (because God also loves this same damned man with infinite love).

God would gladly suffer the pain of hell in his place, says St Catherine of Genoa, if God could suffer.

And God hates the damned man because he loves him and the damned man is his own enemy. God loves what he is or should be, what he ought to *be* in himself, but now he has become a negation of himself, an anti-being. Because sin is the negation of God, it is being an anti-God.

Sin is something that is not, it is something that anti-exists. It is full of emptiness. It is something worse than nothing, because nothingness does not exist, it is nothing, but sin is a real nothingness, a living death. The damned man lives in an eternal state of death and is condemned to be eternally *nothing*.

Physical death is merely the transformation of matter, but eternal death is matter in an eternal corpse-like state. It is a sort of counter-matter, an anti-universe, an anti-creation. Eternal death is the horrible grin of part of the universe turned into a corpse.

The soul in sin is like an extinct star, it is the horror of a vast cold and empty universe where there is no company. God is infinitely good and infinitely beautiful and so sin is the absence of God and the infinite absence of the good and the beautiful and thus infinitely horrible. If God is infinite beauty and goodness, non-God is an infinite horror. And if God is absolute being, sin, which is the negation of God, is absolute non-being, total emptiness and most hideous nothingness. The soul is a being and it cannot stop being, but the soul in sin empty of God is an absolutely cold and empty being, it is totally desolate and full of nothingness.

And the fire of hell is also the fire of love. Hell is a work of divine love, says Dante. Because in hell there is also love, but love without hope. Heaven is requited love, love in possession, hell is disappointed love. The Song of Songs says that jealousy is like the pain of hell; the pain of hell is jealousy. It is loving and being rejected by what you love, it is rejecting love. Anyone who has experienced disappointed love has experienced some of the pain of hell here on earth. Heaven is the communion of saints, and hell is isolation and loneliness. Ontological solitude. The fire of hell is the same fire of concupiscence which sometimes burns in our flesh here on earth. It is selfish love and the burning of desire unsatified and loneliness and jealousy. Hell has a 'material' fire, and we do not know what this fire is like. But in this atomic age we have learnt a little more about the nature of fire. Eternal fire must be an eternal state of molecular or nuclear disintegration of matter. God is love and union, and his love is the force of molecular cohesion in matter, and hell is eternal disintegration, matter falling apart, at war with itself, and the pain of not loving.

Eternity

Death now no longer exists for us. Death for us was baptism, through which we shared in the death of Christ; we died with Christ. Christ died for us and instead of us, and now we need not die. Physical death is merely the beginning of eternal life, 'the condition of resurrection', as Athanasius says. He who has been baptized has passed through death. The other 'death' is not death, but meeting Christ.

Christ is 'the first-born of the dead', as St Paul says. This means Christ was the first (the first-born) to rise again, the first who passed from the womb of death out to the new life, and all those who follow him are like other children, brothers and sisters from the same mother's womb, who follow the first-born down the same birth canal.

Death no longer exists for the monk. He has already overcome it. He who lives in union with God fears nothing, knows that nothing can hurt him now.

Whereas the world's chief concern is the shortness of life, the shortness of time and the speed of days passing is our chief joy. We see time pass like an express train, and we are glad as those are glad who are travelling by train to a longed for destination, a happy meeting. Time is the train speeding to its destination, a train taking us to meet God.

It is not true that life is short. Our life is not short, it is eternal. We do not have death before us, but eternity. We were not born to die, but to live, to live eternally. We do not grieve that time passes so quickly, because life does not pass, only time passes (time which does not exist, the constant passing of the future into the past, and that which is not yet into that which no longer is) and eternity is coming, the ever-present present, without future or past, without end, life in an eternal present, eternal life. We do not fear death because we do not die, we only pass on to a more perfect life, more real, more living, more alive.

Like the caterpillar that falls asleep in its chrysalis and is changed into a butterfly.

'I saw a new heaven and a new earth', says St John in *Revelation*. The cosmos will not perish, there will not be an 'end' of the world, it will be *renewed*. The stars falling means only that there will be a new cosmos, a universe with a new structure. And there will be a new life in this new world.

We belong to this new cosmos, which is already beginning and whose first seed is the risen body of Christ ('the first-born of the dead' and the 'first fruits of the resurrection'). And this seed will grow and multiply till it replaces the old creation ('the kingdom of heaven is like a grain of mustard seed . . .'). Matter will be organized anew in a 'non-corruptible' form, with a new nuclear and cellular structure, and the centre of this new cosmos will be the body of Christ, and all creation will revolve round him as the earth and the planets revolve round the sun. 'And the city has no need of sun or moon to shine upon it, for the glory of God is its light, and its lamp is the lamb.' (Rev. 21.23.) When we take communion with Christ we commune with the resurrection and the renewal of the cosmos ('I am the resurrection and the life'), we drink at the very spring of life.

The cicadas which stay buried in the earth for seventeen years in a larval state and come to life in spring are a symbol of the resurrection of Christ and of our resurrection. Spring which comes every year is also a symbol of this resurrection.

Living

The Christian lives like a traveller, says Clement of Alexandria. We are like tourists who leave a country without great regret because we are going home. We do not leave the world sadly, as if we were going into exile, but gladly like exiles going home, like displaced persons returning.

For those who do not hope for heaven the pleasures and joys of life are sad because they come to an end. Those who hope for heaven are the only ones who can fully enjoy the joys of earth, because they see them as a foretaste of the joys to come, and they are glad that earthly joys pass and quickly come to an end because they long for the joys to come.

Now we see as in a glass, says Paul, but then we shall see face to face and we shall know as we are known. Now we cannot see things in their mysterious essence, as they are known by God, as they are possessed by God, as they are. We only see their images which come to us through our senses, a shape, a colour, a smell, a feel, but not the things themselves. They are merely sense images reflected in our brain. We see 'as in a glass'. But when we see 'face to face' everything will be transformed, our friends, everything round us, the whole world. We shall see them for the first time not through sense images but in the splendour of what they are. We shall know them as they are known by God (because knowing is loving and loving is knowing) and as we ourselves are known and loved by God. And we shall know God as we are known by him, because we shall also see God 'face to face', and not, as we see him now 'in a glass', reflected in things. And when we see God face to face, we shall see things face to face, as they are seen by God, as they are in God, as they are.

We shall see beauty face to face, not the beauty shining through things, but beauty in itself. We shall see it directly, not mediated by things, we shall see beauty, not beautiful things, we shall see without veils, we shall simply see. Heaven is seeing and seeing and also loving and loving and loving. Loving which is seeing and loving which is possessing. And possessing is enjoying. We have tasted joys here on earth, some greater than others, and all these joys are the joy of possessing, but things are limited and so are their joys. But the joy of possessing God is like an immense sea of joy, boundless, bottomless, a joy growing ever greater beyond our utmost capacity for joy.

We shall know as we are known. We shall possess God as we are possessed by God, we shall be owners of God as he is our owner, we shall enjoy God, as God enjoys, we shall be God as God is God. Because seeing God is possessing God and possessing God is being like God. 'We shall be like him because we shall see him as he is', says St John (First letter, 3.2).

And then we shall know each other for the first time and heaven will be a communion of love. Because here on earth we cannot know each other well, we only know by appearances, and even those who know and love each other best are always a profound mystery to one another, always fundamentally unknown, just as we are unknown to our-

selves and are a mystery to ourselves. Only in heaven shall
we truly communicate with one another, only in heaven
can we speak our utmost word, and we shall have no need
of language because we shall have a perfect communion of
love. Time will be over, says Revelation. There will no
longer be the torment of time passing, the party ending,
and we shall not know each other piecemeal as we know
each other now in time, like an ever-rolling stream. We
shall know each other with total knowledge, in the total
presence of those we love. The things we say now are
blown away on the wind, smiles fade, and the joy of being
with the person we love does not last. Time blows it away
like smoke on the wind. But in heaven there will be neither
space nor time. We shall love in eternity, in eternal life, life
which is movement, but movement which does not pass
away, eternal presence. And there will no longer be the torment of space. Now we can never be with all the people we
like at the same time. To be with some we must be absent
from others, and there are so many others whom we do not
even know, whom we might also like, just as those we now
like and are friends with were once unknown and strangers
to us. But in heaven we shall all be together, and we shall
enjoy the company of all those we now partly know and
love and all those others we do not love because we do not
know them. Then we shall be close to all humanity, and
how great the love will be between those who now love
each other here in the changes and chances of space and
time, who are close to one another. We shall see again those
who have died, those we saw grow old and die, and those
who grew old with us. We shall see them all again and no
body on earth is as beautiful as their bodies will be then.
The beauty of the human body can give us an idea of what

the splendour of the resurrection will be, of what heaven will be. As Novalis said, touching a human body is a bit like touching heaven. But beauty grows old. And this beauty is to the risen body as the seed is to the plant, says Paul (1 Cor. 15.35–50). So what can money, success or pleasure matter to us, when we think of heaven? We no longer fear death, we desire it. We do not grieve for the death of others, we envy them, because we want to get to heaven as quickly as possible. It does not sadden us to grow old. We want to die soon or grow old soon. We want life to fly past (and indeed it does) and for space and time to be over soon, pleasures which come to an end, absences, disappointments, pain, disaster, sickness, death and the fear of death.

Paradise

God set an angel with a fiery sword at the gate of Paradise, and from then on there was sadness and boredom in all pleasure.

Ever since man was turned out of Paradise he has been trying to get back. Childhood, spring, the discovery of love are like remnants of Paradise. And the innocence of animals, which they did not lose.

But Paradise is not to be found in the tropics, as Columbus believed. It is not to be found in the 'tropical paradises' advertised by travel agencies. Neither at Florida Springs nor at Miami Beach. Paradise is on Calvary. 'Today you will be with me in Paradise.' The thief had spoken to Christ of his kingdom. 'Remember me when you come into your kingdom.' Christ answered him with the word 'Paradise': 'Today you will be with me in Paradise.' He meant that he was reopening the gates of paradise for us.

It was not a metaphor, because at the time he was dying on the cross and talking to another dying man. It was not the right moment for metaphor. Those who have accepted the cross and gone up Mount Calvary know quite well that it is not a metaphor.

From then on Paradise has been open to us again. But Paradise is not to be found in pleasure, or in comfort or in tropical 'paradise' hotels, or at Miami Beach. It is to be found on Calvary.

Paradise is union with God. Eve comes out of Christ's wounded side, just as she once came from Adam's rib. And Adam cries again: 'This at last is bone of my bones and flesh of my flesh ... therefore a man leaves his father and mother and cleaves to his wife.'

Union with God makes the earth a paradise once more. Where God is with me, there is paradise and the whole of nature is the lovely backcloth to our friendship, the starry sky, mountains, apple tree in blossom.

Nature is no longer hostile to him who lives in the presence of God. He feels safe from all harm, just as Adam did in Paradise. Without God's presence we feel danger all round us, that at any time things can wound, crush, suffocate, mutilate, batter or bite us. But he who lives in union with God knows that a leaf does not fall without God's consent and that every hair of his head is counted, that no creature has power to harm him.

For him who lives in union with God all things are transfigured by a special light and joy springs from them, even the most common everyday things. Blessedness falls on every moment of his life and there is a kind of enchantment upon everything he touches, everything he does. As Christ said to the woman at the well, the water that I shall give him will become in him a spring of water welling up to eternal life. ('And the woman said to him, "Sir, give me this water, that I may not thirst, nor come here to draw." ')

Paradise is love. Every lover feels that he has spent a little time in paradise, but he who lives in the love of God lives in paradise all the time.

Every human love is a glimpse of eternity. But a fleeting eternity. Eternity is glimpsed in this fleeting because God's life is also motion but eternal motion, an infinite present which never passes away, whereas in human love we seize for a moment an eternity which does pass away. Human love is a brief eternity but the joy of God is an eternal movement, because God's eternity is not static but eternal life, and he is the source of life and life is movement.

Human love took over the language of mystical love, says Bergson, not mystical love the language of human love.

In modern times marriage is thought of as a mystical union, and the modern girl comes to her wedding with the same expectations as the Christian virgin when she became the bride of Christ. Commercial propaganda shows domestic life as a kind of paradise on earth. The husband or wife is expected to be a god or a goddess, which is why there is so much frustration in so many marriages today. Creatures are required to give what only God can give. Wife and home are expected to satisfy an infinite thirst for love which only God can satisfy.

Fame & knowing

We want to be known. Ants happily pass their days climbing up and down a plant stalk, quite content with the tiny corner of creation God has allotted them. They do not want to be well known or famous. They are content to be the anonymous creatures God created them, content just to be. They are known by God and that is enough. But we feel that if we live an 'obscure' life, unknown to the world, it is like not existing.

The spider spinning her web does not want publicity. The small insect does not sign its autograph, but a film star in all her finery is not clothed so gloriously. The cardinal bird flies swiftly through the wood shunning all publicity. It tries to conceal, not show off its beauty. And the rabbit runs through the wood and hides, and is content with its hidden life. But you do not want an 'obscure' life. You want to be known.

It is true that to be known is to be, and that is why we want to be known (and if we are unknown we feel like shadows). Eternal glory is called glory because it is like human glory, it means being known. But human glory is a false glory, because it means being known by people who are not any more than we are, and their knowledge of us does not affect our being. We are no less if we lead an obscure life unknown to the world. We are no more if we are famous with the fame given by a publicity agent and if our names appear in newspaper headlines and we are interviewed on radio and television.

Our true existence lies in being known by God. We are to the extent that we are known by God. Not being known by God is not being, because he knows everything. But God does not know evil because he is infinitely innocent.

That is why Francis of Assisi so often repeated: 'I am what I am before God.' And Christ says that God rejects those whom he does not admit to the kingdom of heaven with the words: 'I do not know you.'

Our desire for fame comes from our vague realization that we do not fully exist if we do not exist in the mind of Someone outside ourselves. And we feel that being unknown is like not being. But fame among men does not make us immortal, for they too are mortal and need to be in the mind of others in order to be, otherwise they too are shadows. Our reality thus depends on other shadows and we think we are real because we are reflected in the unreality of others, we are shadows of shadows. That is why human glory is but a shadow.

But heaven also means knowing. 'I shall know as I am known,' says Paul. Heaven is seeing. It is contemplation and vision. Our reward will be seeing, says Augustine. Because seeing and understanding and grasping are possessing ('knowing' in the biblical sense) and also loving. Seeing is receiving and just as through our sight and our other senses we receive the perceptible reality round us, so seeing God is receiving God and possessing him. And seeing God is also being like God. 'We shall be like him because we shall see him as he is.' (1 John 3.2.)

Contemplating God is being like God because we are

natural imitators and to see God is to imitate him. We become more and more like God throughout eternity. That is why a soul which sees God *is* God.

The soul is essentially a mirror, and so not something valuable in itself (just as the mirror in itself is just glass), but for the beauty reflected in it. The soul's beauty is the beauty of God reflected in it. And the soul without God is a mirror with nothing reflected in it. It is a thing which is not.

Man by nature is a thirst for knowledge, understanding and possession, and this thirst is for God.

To know God is what we seek in journeys, in science, in books, in love. This is why we thirst for experience and our thirst can only be satisfied by God. Theresa of Lisieux looked forward to heaven, thinking that there she would understand how birds, and flowers and the wind are made. Know, know, know.

But then we shall not know reality in a limited way, through our five senses, as we do now. We shall know total reality, as it is, with a direct knowledge, with the knowledge —in the biblical sense—of loving possession.

Or, as César Vallejo said: 'The kisses will be given that you could not give.'

Evolution

Bees give honey to man and silk worms clothe him, but the chief service done by plants and animals to man is not that they feed and clothe him, not that they serve other animals which in turn serve man, but that they passed life on to him, they are his forerunners in the long process of evolution. They are part of man and are called to share with us in the resurrection. The fossilized trilobite that lived five hundred million years ago did not die altogether but he passed on life to our bodies and in a way it is still living in our bodies and waiting for the resurrection with us.

We are organically connected with all creation and when Adam sinned, the whole of nature was cursed because of him. 'Cursed be the earth because of you,' God told him. And at the flood God did not repent only of having made man but also all creation. 'I will blot out man whom I have created from the face of the ground, man and beast and creeping things, and birds of the air.' Because through man 'the earth was filled with violence' and 'all flesh had corrupted their way upon the earth'. And God's rainbow covenant with Noah after the flood was a covenant with all creation. 'This is the sign of the covenant which I make between me and you and every living creature that is with you.' And in the same way Christ's new covenant is not only with men but with all creatures. And when Christ rose from the dead he told his apostles to preach the gospel to *every* creature (not men alone). And all creatures groan with us in labour, in expectation of the resurrection.

Because all creatures on earth are related through biological evolution, the resurrection of the body is but one stage further, the last stage in this process of evolution. With the resurrection of Christ this final stage has already begun. Christ is the first specimen of this new 'biological' era or, as Paul said, 'the first-born' and the 'first fruits of the resurrection'. Our resurrection is like one more metamorphosis, and the metamorphoses of living things through the pre-Cambrian, the Cambrian, the Silurian, the Devonian, the Palaeozoic and the Mesozoic periods, towards us can help us to imagine this further transformation (or, as Paul says, we have only to consider the metamorphosis of a grain of wheat).

Every birth is painful for every birth is also a death. Coming out of his mother's womb means the death of his former life to the child, it is the end of his comfortable foetal existence and that is why he cries when he is born. And all the other stages of growth are further painful deaths which each of us must suffer. 'Unless a grain of wheat falls into the earth and dies, it remains alone, but if it dies it bears much fruit.' (John 12.24.) And unless the cell subdivides it remains alone, but if it subdivides it bears much fruit. And the stars too are like grains of wheat. They too are born through painful deaths. They are produced by great explosions.

The whole cosmos is like a great grain of wheat. And like the child in its mother's womb, it is waiting to be born. It groans with labour pains.

This new birth is also painful and we resist it because we

are very comfortable as we are enclosed in our present cosmos. It is like the warm darkness of our mother's womb, where we sleep more than live and we do not want to be born and go out into life. But the life process must go on and we must go on to the new life or die. As Christ said to Nicodemus: 'Unless a man is born again he cannot enter the kingdom of God.'

Christ is the first-born ('the first-born of the dead'). The empty tomb on the morning of the resurrection was like a womb newly delivered of its first child. Some of the matter of which we are made (calcium, iron, phosphorus, potassium) has left our universe and now belongs to a new creation. There has been an empty space in the matter of the universe ever since the tomb was found empty on the morning of the resurrection. Or as the proper for the Ascension says, 'Set at the right hand of thy glory the substance of our frail human nature'. Frail human biology at God's right hand, and us too as sharers in that biology.

It is a natural biological process, as the parable clearly said: 'And he said: "The kingdom of God is as if a man should scatter seed upon the ground, and should sleep and rise night and day, and the seed should sprout and grow, he knows not how. The earth produces of itself, first the blade, then the ear, then the full grain in the ear. But when the grain is ripe, at once he puts in the sickle because the harvest has come".' (Mark. 4.26–9.)

And the harvest will come sooner than we think. The prophet Amos says that in those days he that is still ploughing will see the reaper right behind him.

Man more human

Christ told us in many parables that the kingdom of heaven is an evolutionary process. It is a grain of wheat, a seed which the sower goes out to sow, a leaven which a woman puts in a lump of dough, a grain of mustard seed which when it is sown is the smallest of all seeds but when it grows becomes one of the largest shrubs and the birds of the air find shelter in its branches. He used similes from nature and ordinary life to tell us that the kingdom of heaven belongs to the same process as nature and ordinary life. And at the same time he wanted to tell us that the kingdom of heaven is a slow process, as the formation of the stars was a slow process through billions and billions of years, and the formation of the earth through long geological ages—during which the kingdom of heaven was already beginning to be formed on earth—and as the mustard seed grows slowly, and the grain of wheat.

The cosmos is not made only of space but also of time, or space which is time. If we lift our eyes to the stars we see them not only through space but also through time. And if we look with a telescope at the furthest stars, our telescope takes us not only through space but also through time and we see something that existed aeons ago.

This time dimension which we find in all the universe is also like a parable of the kingdom of heaven. 'If you had as

much faith as a grain of mustard seed,' said Christ on
another occasion. And we know that the mustard seed con-
tains locked up and folded up inside it the mustard bush.
And that all biological evolution was contained in the first
cell. We have the seeds. They do not look much. But faith
takes a handful of ugly, wrinkled, dried out seeds . . .

And there is a hidden mystery in these parables about
seeds: seeds belong to evolution. We are descended from
them or rather we are the final development of these same
seeds and together with all the other beings in the animal
and vegetable kingdom we form the tree of life. The kingdom of heaven is not only like a seed, it *is* a seed (the first
cell grew and multiplied until it became corn and the first
mustard bush and then man within whom is contained—as
in a seed—the kingdom of heaven). And just as the grain of
wheat and the mustard seed and the cell must divide in
order to reproduce itself, so man must die in order to grow,
to form the complete man, or the mystical body, the
fulness of the stature of the body of Christ, as Paul says.
And within this mystical body, all living beings are contained, our genealogical tree, as the birds of heaven shelter
in the mustard tree. Because the kingdom of heaven is
evolution. It is a biological continuation of the mineral
kingdom and the vegetable kingdom and the animal kingdom and also of human kingdoms, of human socialization
or hominization, as Teilhard de Chardin says.

The Jews expected the kingdom of God to be an earthly
kingdom, and in this they were not mistaken because the
kingdom of heaven is also earthly, it is the kingdom of
heaven established on earth and that is why we pray for it
to come to us in the Our Father. The kingdom of heaven is
a kingdom—or as we should say nowadays a republic—that

is, a social order. The kingdom of heaven is social, an *ecclesia*, a community, a spiritual marxism. But the Jews (like Marxists today) were mistaken in thinking it was a social order like those already existing on earth because, as Christ said to Pilate, his kingdom is not of this world, it is of a different order. As he said to his apostles: 'The kings of the Gentiles exercise lordship over them; and those in authority over them are called benefactors. But not so with you; rather let the greatest among you become as the youngest, and the leader as one who serves.' (Lk. 22.25–6.) That is to say, the order is reversed. It is a kingdom without subjects, a democratic kingdom, a nation of kings, as St Peter says (1 Pet. 2.9). Isaiah had prophesied this kingdom as a real social order, a new order which men would bring here on earth: 'The wolf shall dwell with the lamb and the leopard shall lie down with the kid, and the calf and the lion and the fatling together, and a little child shall lead them. The cow and the bear shall feed; their young shall lie down together; and the lion shall eat straw like the ox. The sucking child shall play over the hole of the asp, and the weaned child shall put his hand on the adder's den.' (Isaiah 11.6–8.)

Christ came on earth to establish this kingdom. It is already established in a small way, in religious communities, in monasteries, under artificial conditions as in a laboratory. Monasteries are trying out the social system of the future, but Christ did not come to establish his kingdom only in the laboratory, in monasteries. He came to make his kingdom the social system of villages, of nations, of humanity. The Church is humanity. And the present Church is the small seemingly insignificant seed of this humanity. That is why the kingdom of heaven is like a grain of mustard seed.

Man & universe

When you look at the universe on a starry night (our galaxy has three hundred thousand million stars, stars with the brightness of three hundred thousand suns and there are a hundred million galaxies in the universe to be explored), you should not feel your littleness and insignificance but your greatness. For the human spirit is much greater than these universes. Because we can look at these worlds and understand them and be aware of them, but they cannot understand us. These worlds are made up of simple molecules, like the hydrogen molecule which has just one nucleus and one electron. But the human body is made of more complicated molecules and also has life which is of a complexity far beyond the molecular world. We also have consciousness and love. And when a lover says that the eyes of his beloved are brigher than stars, this is no exaggeration (even though Sigma of the Dorado is three hundred thousand times brighter than the sun) because the light of intelligence and love shines in her eyes and not in Sigma of the Dorado, Alpha of the Lyra or Antares. And even were the radius of the universe a hundred thousand million light years, the radius of the universe is still limited. And the humblest of men is greater than the whole material universe. His greatness is of another order beyond mere size. For the whole material universe can be contained as a small point in the human mind which is thinking of it.

And these worlds are dumb. They praise God, but with unconscious praise. They do not know they are doing it. And you are the voice of these worlds and their awareness. But these worlds are not capable of love, whereas you are.

But your mind is not separate from these worlds. You are also this vast universe. You are its mind and heart. You are the vast universe thinking and loving.

The human soul completes the universe, as Plato says. It was created so that the cosmos might have a mind. Man is the perfection of the visible creation and we cannot think him low and vile ('vile worm of the earth'), for this would mean calling all God's work low and vile.

And the vastness of the universe you see on a starry night becomes even greater if you think of yourself too as part of this same universe, and realize that you are the universe itself thinking of itself, and that as well as its dimensions of time and space it has in you a further dimension which is even greater.

We are the mind of the cosmos. And the incarnation of the Word in a human body means his incarnation into the whole cosmos.

For the whole cosmos is in communion. The calcium that is in our bodies is the same calcium that is in the sea (and we took it from the sea because our life came from the sea). And the calcium of our bodies and of the sea is the same as the calcium of the sky, the stars' calcium and the calcium floating in the interstellar oceans from which the stars came (for the stars are a concentration of the thin matter in the interstellar spaces and came from them just as our bodies came from the sea). And in fact there is no emptiness between the stars and the galaxies. The whole universe is really a single mass of matter, more or less rarefied or concentrated and the whole cosmos is a single body. The elements of meteorites come from far off stars (calcium, iron, copper, phosphorus) are the same as the elements of our planet, of our body, and the same as the elements of the interstellar spaces. So we are made of star, or rather the cosmos is made of our own flesh. And when the Word was made flesh and dwelt among us, he could have said of all nature, as Adam said of Eve: 'This now is flesh of my flesh and bone of my bones.' In Christ's body, as in ours, there is all creation. And the whole creation is also in the mystical body of Christ, which is all of us and all creation too.

In our bodies all living animals and all fossils are in communion with each other, and the metals and the elements of the universe. The sculptor working in stone is made of the same matter as the stone. He is like the mind of the stone, the stone turned artist. He is matter plus soul. And when we love God and are united with him, all creation and all its kingdoms, animal, vegetable and mineral, love God and are united with him too.

Nature is far more sacred to the Christian than it could have been to the pagan pantheist. We are more than pantheists because Christianity transcends pantheism and the incarnation goes further than the wildest dreams of all the philosophers and all the pantheists.

Our bodies are sacred. They are temples, says Paul (and for the Jews nothing was more sacred than the temple), and all nature shares in our bodies' holiness. All creation is a temple, says Gregory the Great. Trees, stones, lizards, rabbits, meteors, comets and stars to us are holy.

Singing in the night

Nature is constantly communing with itself. It is always eating itself and offering itself to be eaten. Food is the communion of life. Food is not 'prosaic'. The Creator willed that in order to live we must eat other living beings because he wanted living beings to be in communion with one another. He did not want us to be independent of one another and self, sufficient. He wanted us to need to assimilate other living beings all the time and that through this assimilation we should remain in communion with the whole cosmos. The copepod eats the diatom and the herring the copepod and the squid the herring and the perch the squid and when the perch dies and decays it in turn feeds the diatom or is eaten by humans and human remains feed the diatom, for life and death are all one, and life is constantly being reborn from itself. We should not worry about imagining the resurrection of the flesh because our flesh will have gone on to become the flesh of other beings, because in this very process we are seeing the resurrection of the flesh already at work. With what body shall we rise? We shall rise with all bodies and all ages, or rather one single body will rise again, with many ages. In it we shall all be flesh of others and within one another as the foetus is in its mother. Only those who are not saved will be outside this body, and so the damnation of one person mutilates the body of Christ. And this is why Paul says that all creation, including plants and animals, is groaning in expectation of the resurrection of our body. And so only one body need rise to make it necessary that all bodies should rise. It is enough that Christ has risen—'the first born from the dead'—to make it necessary for all creation to rise again.

Christ redeemed not only human nature but all nature. Bread and wine and water were also redeemed and through Christ all matter has become holy and sacramental. Even the birds and the fishes of the sea share in the holiness of Christ and our holiness. Mother Nature became holy together with Mary the mother of Christ, for we are all in holy communion, from the lowliest invertebrates and mammals to the mother of God, and the humblest mammals also share in Mary's motherhood.

When we commune with Christ the whole cosmos communes with us. The Mayans believed that man was made of maize because they had an inkling of this communion and this mystical body. And Mayan sacrifices and all pagan eucharists were also a dark and imperfect sharing in this cosmic communion, this mystical body (for as the Lord said to the Jews through the mouth of the prophet Malachi, he received sacrifices not only from Israel but also from all the pagan peoples on earth: 'For from the rising of the sun to its setting my name is great among the nations, and in every place incense is offered to my name, and a pure offering; for my name is great among the nations, says the Lord of hosts.' Mal. 1.11).

Christ chose bread and wine for the Eucharist because these were the basic food and drink in the Mediterranean culture which was the most universal at the time, and so they were the most universal food and drink (and wheat is the cereal grown most of throughout the planet) but the bread and wine of the Eucharist represent all the fruits of the earth, maize, cocoa, coffee, tobacco, bananas, coconuts, pulque and chicha.

And every fruit is like a synthesis of the whole cosmos, it is an assimilable chunk of cosmic matter, just as the bread and wine of the mass are a synthesis and represent the whole cosmos. And they also represent our bodies for our bodies are also fruits; we are these fruits assimilated and turned into bodies. Our flesh and blood are bread and wine. And when the bread and wine are changed into the body and blood of Christ, they symbolize our body and blood changed into the body and blood of Christ.

We all share in the same cosmic rhythm. The rotation of atoms and the circulation of our blood and the sap running through plants and the tides of the sea and the phases of the moon and the rotation of the stars in the galaxy and the rotation of the galaxies. It is all the same rhythm, all the same song, sung in chorus by the whole universe. For all natural laws, as the Book of Wisdom says, are like the rhythm of the strings of the harp. And the singing of monks and the liturgical cycle following the cycle of seed-time and harvest and the seasons of the year, and the cycle of life and death (and the life and death and resurrection of Christ) are part of this cosmic rhythm. It is a human sharing in the rhythm of the sea and the moon and animal breeding and the stars. And pagan liturgies also followed the harvest cycle and the seasons and joined in the cosmic rhythm which modern man in the cities has lost. For this rhythm is religion. As oysters depend on the rhythm of the sea for their breeding and the palolos in the southern seas

depend on the moon, man depends on ritual and the
liturgical cycle. For as Ecclesiasticus says, it is religion
which gives rhythm to human life. 'Why does one day ex-
cel another, when all the light of every day in the year is
of the sun? By the knowledge of the Lord they were distin-
guished; and he altered seasons and feasts.' (Ecclesiasticus
33.7–9.) And that is why life in cities like New York is so
horribly monotonous.

That is why our religion is catholic, that is to say, universal, not just because it is the religion of all men but because
it is the religion of the whole cosmos. It reaches from molluscs to the stars, it embraces all other rites and all that was
true in all the ancient pagan religions, and it embraces
more than religion—in the conventional sense of the word.
It embraces the whole man (with his poetry, his painting,
his folklore, his dances, his seedtime and harvest festivals,
and the growth of plants and animals and the love between
men and women), and outside this religion there is no
salvation.

The whole universe is a song, a song in chorus, a festive
song, of the wedding feast ('A king made a wedding feast
for his son'). We have not yet arrived at the feast but we
have been invited, and we see the light and hear the music
from afar. 'But at midnight there was a cry, "Behold, the
bridegroom! Come out to meet him".' (Mt. 25.6.) And John
the Baptist also proclaimed his arrival, and pointed him
out: 'He who has the bride is the bridegroom: the friend
of the bridegroom who stands and hears him rejoices
greatly at the bridegroom's voice.' (John 3.29.) The liturgy is
the daily commemoration, here on earth and in time, of this
wedding feast which has already begun in eternity. So for
the Catholic Church all days are feast days and in the

liturgy all the days are called *feria*, which means feast (the feast of Monday, the feast of Tuesday, and so on) and every day of the zodiacal and liturgical year is for us a symbol of the eternal feast which never ends. And our song, together with the chorus of stars and atoms is the same as the angels' chorus and the same as the song that may be sung by countless other spiritual races on countless other planets, to which the Book of Job seems to refer when it speaks of the morning stars singing together and the sons of God shouting with joy. We are still in the darkness awaiting the bridegroom, but we already see the light far away and hear singing in the night.